FINDINGBETTER

FINDING A BETTER YOU...

—

FREE OF DEPRESSION.

—

FREE OF ANXIETY.

BEN CHAMPION

FINDING BETTER

First Print Edition

Copyright © 2019 Ben Champion.

ISBN: 9781075794889 (Paperback)

Front cover and design by Ben Champion.
Main Font Used: Book Antiqua—a Roman typeface designed by Monotype Inc.

Published and printed by *Amazon Publishing Services*, Inc., in the United States of America.
Amazon Services LLC: 410 Terry Ave N, Seattle, WA 98109

Find more at: www.findingbetter.org
Instagram: @ThisIsFindingBetter
Email: connect@findingbetter.org

READ THIS FIRST

Who should read this book?

More and more young adults are struggling with **Depression** and **Anxiety**. *FINDING BETTER* helps them **overcome** these challenges to find a **better** version of themselves...

If that sounds like what you are looking for — a way to *find better* — then you've found the right book.

There are many levels of Depression and Anxiety. As much as this book is written for those going through a serious season of struggle, it's also intended to help anyone feeling these challenges at any level.

In fact, I think a large portion of our generation is facing Depression and Anxiety on a moderate level. Many young adults are feeling the effects of low-grade Depression and Anxiety play out in their lives. Worried and unsettled, dissatisfied and disheartened, our generation is good at covering up the feelings of mediocrity that can weigh heavily on us. It may not be a level of Depression or Anxiety that's fully *debilitating*, but *disrupting*... absolutely!

Staying in this state keeps us from *finding better* and as a result, from *living* better.

My story is one of facing Depression and Anxiety on all levels at some point. Regardless of the severity, the solution is the same: a deliberate choice to seek change and intentionally *find better*.

If Depression or Anxiety is not your struggle, then you likely have a friend or family member who's facing these challenges. Press into this book! Choose to intentionally direct the words on each page toward them. Your impact on their life will be more powerful than you could ever imagine.

If you're like me, then you flip through books and start reading random chapters that seem most interesting to you. Rarely do I have the patience to read an entire book. So, if that's you, I feel ya! However, this book has a unique structure. Some sections are best read in order, and others, not necessarily. Here's the breakdown so that you can get the most out of the content.

PART I: Begin with this, and read it in order. This is the foundation for the entire book.

PARTS II & III: Each chapter talks about a specific subject matter. Feel free to bounce around and read in any order that seems most intriguing to you. (Think of it like blog meets book.)

PART IV: This is a spiritual section. It's best to read it all together, in order, since it pertains to one topic. If you're not interested in that subject matter, then skip it.

PART V: This section is best after reading some or all of the earlier chapters. It brings all of the content together.

There's no pressure to read this book cover to cover. Take your own path at your own pace. This is about *you* finding a better version of yourself.

TABLE OF CONTENTS

FINDINGBETTER.

If you look carefully at the cover of this book, you'll see a winding road that's heading off in an unknown direction. Figuratively speaking, we choose the roads we travel on in life—the directions we take. Many times, we find ourselves far down the wrong road before we realize that the path we're on isn't fulfilling. Somewhere, we must have taken a wrong turn.

You may not like the road you're currently on. It may seem pitted with struggle, cracked by pain, covered with insecurities, or just seemingly insignificant. However, picking up this book, and your decision to pivot, is the beginning of choosing a new road. This road will uncover joy, peace, and confidence; replacing Depression, Anxiety, and insecurity. Before you know it, you'll be on a path that can only be described by one simple word: **Better.**

As a start to this journey, I have a story to share…

PART I

A STARTING POINT

JUST A SMALL BUMP
· I N T R O D U C T I O N ·

Can you think of a time when you went through something so embarrassing or so frustrating that it's permanently embedded in your memory? Well for me, having my wisdom teeth removed is an experience I'll never forget.

For some reason, I've always had terrible teeth issues. Going back to elementary school, the gap between my two front teeth was so big that I could fit a #2 pencil in between them. As a third-grader, I found this to be a pretty neat talent, and so did my friends. However, as I grew up, I became self-conscious about the gap that I once used to impress. All of a sudden, "middle school Ben" didn't want crooked, wide-spaced teeth anymore. I mean come on... how was I supposed to ask my crush to the Fall Dance with a smile looking like a jack- o'-lantern?

So, I begged my parents to let me start braces.

My orthodontic experience took a total of ten months with an expander, three years with traditional braces, hundreds of tiny glow-in-the-dark rubber bands (if you know, you know), two years of wearing an "after braces" special retainer, a pulled tooth, and the addition of an artificial implant. Let me tell ya, it was one looonnng process to get a set of pearly whites!

At that point, I thought I was in the clear. Done with dental work.

But, not just yet...

When I turned 20, my dentist informed me that it was time to remove my wisdom teeth. Flashbacks of my insane journey to a decent smile haunted me as he spoke the words, "Let's set up an appointment to have them removed."

He reassured me that it was a simple procedure. Friends and family backed up his optimistic claim.

The time came for me to have my surgery and surprisingly, it went smoothly.

The following days were spent binge-watching *The Office* and deliberately eating several pints of "Seven Layer Bar" Ben and Jerry's ice cream. After a few days, I was feeling much better. I honestly thought, "Well maybe they were right, it wasn't that bad."

Boy, was I wrong!

A week later, a small bump began forming on my jawline. At first, I barely even noticed it. I thought it was probably insignificant swelling from the healing process. But within 24 hours, the tiny bump expanded into a big, painful lump on the right side of my cheek. Imagine the "Everlasting Gobstopper" from *Charlie and the Chocolate Factory* dreadfully squished between my gum and lower jaw.

NO, PLEASE NOOOO! ARE YOU KIDDING ME! WHAT DID I DO TO DESERVE THIS?

I rushed in to have the dentist check on it, and he informed me that the strange lump was a result of the surgery. He claimed, "This rarely happens! I'll prescribe you some antibiotics and an antiseptic mouthwash, and it should slowly clear up."

The worst part was that I was planning on going to a young adult retreat the following weekend. It was a great opportunity to make new friends and experience some much-needed adventure in my life. But, how was I supposed to enjoy a retreat, much less, meet other young adults, when I looked like a blowfish?

I had a choice to make: Either bail on the retreat, or forge ahead and get past my misshaped face. I remember asking my mom, "Will I ever feel like me again?"

I decided that I'd rather be uncomfortable than miss the opportunities that the weekend had in store.

The retreat didn't disappoint. It turned out to be an amazing experience that not only refreshed my soul, but led me to finding lifelong friends.

Shortly after, my mouth did heal. I questioned the timing of it all, but came to the conclusion that I actually wouldn't have had it any other way. That weekend challenged me to develop new levels of self-confidence. I pushed myself to start conversations with new people. I pushed myself to show up to all of the activities. And, I pushed myself to use the world's worst mouthwash three-times daily!

All this to say:

Sometimes, just showing up is a victory…

By deciding to read this book, you're "showing up." That's a victory in and of itself.

And yet, this is just one step of many that will take you in a new direction.

WILL I EVER FEEL LIKE ME AGAIN?

· A STARTING POINT ·

In my life, I've asked my parents twice, "Will I ever feel like me again?" Once was during my painful wisdom teeth ordeal, and before that, right after my first year of college. While the experience with my wisdom teeth merited that question, in hindsight, it now seems insignificant and even a little bit laughable. However, when I asked them, "Will I ever feel like me again" after my first year of college... *I desperately meant it.* I was *fragile, broken,* and *lost* after two emotionally draining semesters.

After a period of consistently living with poor lifestyle choices, combined with confronting many challenges all young adults face, I found myself in a terrible season of Depression and Anxiety. Some triggers were self-induced, and some were out of my control.

It was a mixture of…
- regularly partying
- leaving my home, and with it, family and friends
- wrestling to find an authentic identity
- perpetuating the social priorities of my previous friend group
- progressively struggling with acne (resulting in extremely low self-confidence)
- difficulty adapting to a new environment
- increasing academic pressures
- an inability (and prideful resistance) to label my feelings
- failing to maintain a long-distance relationship with a girl I loved, which led to a devastating breakup

Each of these pieces played a part in the forming of my "perfect storm."

As I approached the second semester of my freshman year, it all came to a head as I started experiencing weekly panic attacks. I began having trouble getting through each day, dealing with substantial insecurities and persistent Depression and Anxiety. I'd make it through my classes and then come right back to my room, just wanting to shut down. I felt so self-conscious that I was distracted during most conversations. Many nights ended in tears, feeling inadequate, not like myself, and heavily discouraged. I had never felt the emotions that I was increasingly feeling (or at least with that intensity and frequency). I felt unable to handle life, much less, interested in trying. I ended up having to leave school early to come back home to Colorado where I was (1) close to family and, (2) in an environment more conducive for healing.

When I got back, I initially thought that if I could just find "me" again—the version of myself who had previously struggled less—then I'd be okay. But, I needed to find more than just "me" again. I needed to find an entirely new, more fully equipped version of myself.

I needed to *find better*.

My process of *finding better* was not a quick one, but over the next year, I consistently took steps in a new direction.

I've since found that my story and my troubles aren't uncommon. I once thought my situation was unique to me until I began hearing numerous family and friends—and many 20-somethings—open up about facing similar difficulties. It quickly became apparent that my struggles resonated with challenges our generation and culture are increasingly dealing with.

With that realization, I don't doubt that your life may be presenting many challenges too—forming a similar storm-like condition that you're trying to navigate.

———————————

When I went through my lowest season, I wished I had a resource that *outlined*, *defined*, and *directed* the steps I needed to take to *find better*. I realized that there was a critical need for a book that gave my peers a powerful toolbox of solutions when faced with Depression or Anxiety. A book that would offer specific, tailored advice that was *relatable* and *easy to digest*. That's why I decided to write this—so that you (or someone you know) can better understand and overcome these challenges to find a *better* version of yourself.

———————————

The American College Health Association reported that at some point, "40% of college students have felt so depressed it was difficult to function," and "over 60% have felt overwhelming Anxiety."[1] Adding to that, another study found that there's been a "30 percent rise in students seeking appointments at counseling centers" over the last decade.[2]

Yet still, our natural tendency is to deny that (1) we might be struggling, (2) our actions could be affecting our stability and, (3) the way we're feeling should be taken seriously and addressed.

It took almost seven months of struggling before I spoke the words, "I might be depressed. I might be anxious." That's because both Depression and Anxiety have such a strong, negative stigma. There's a "shhhhhh, don't talk about it" effect. And many people (including naïve 19-year-old Ben Champion), don't even believe that either Depression or Anxiety are real or serious. There may even be someone reading this who hasn't yet labeled what they're going through and feeling as Depression or Anxiety.

Many times, Depression and Anxiety *are* triggered by a certain situation, e.g., losing your job, a divorce/breakup, bullying/harassment, moving, financial burdens, a reaction to a medication, or a tragic loss. However, both Depression and Anxiety aren't necessarily situational. Many people feel the presence of one or the other, or both, *even when their life seems externally steady*. Sadly, if they have the courage to speak up about their feelings, their vulnerability is often met with someone saying, "What do you mean? You have nothing to be anxious or depressed about. You have a great life. Just focus on being more content, happy, calm, busy," and the list goes on. For this reason and many others, people try to ignore and suppress their struggles, only to have them build up even more over time.

You may think that you need an explanation for why you feel the way you do, but I'm here to tell you, you don't. At the same time, that reality isn't an excuse to put off pursuing "better." There's always work that can be done and new approaches that can be taken.

———————

A year or so after my lowest season, I heard a speaker named Chad Bruegman label Depression and Anxiety as "equal opportunity offenders."[3] He spoke about the complexities of both, and how they can reach people in all stages of life. "Equal opportunity offender" means that both Depression and Anxiety can affect anyone. It doesn't matter how old you are, what your race is, how much money you make, or how attractive you may be. It doesn't matter whether or not you're a gifted athlete or a dedicated artist. Nor does it matter if you live on the warm coast of California, or in the dense urban environment of New York City. Neither Depression nor Anxiety have bias. They're *equal opportunity offenders.*

Mirroring his point, what do these men and women have in common?

- An author who has sold over 400 million books
- The most Grammy-nominated woman in music history
- A five-time NBA All-Star and League Champion
- A man who's literally known by the nickname, "The Rock"
- And we can't forget, the talent behind Michael Scott (the manager of *Dunder Mifflin*; Scranton, PA's top regional paper supply company)

The surprising answer…

JK Rowling, Beyoncé, Kevin Love, Dwayne "The Rock" Johnson, and Steve Carell have all opened up about seasons in their life when they have battled Depression or Anxiety.

Other well-known figures/influencers such as Adele, Kristin Bell, Ellen Degeneres, Cara Delevingne, Chip Gaines, Selena Gomez, Joseph Gordon-Levitt, Dan Harris, Anne Hathaway, Lewis Howes, Brad Pitt, Amanda Seyfried, Emma Stone, Channing Tatum, Serena Williams, and Oprah Winfrey have all struggled as well.

I don't know about you, but if I possessed the athletic abilities, the linguistic creativity, or the swagger and confidence that some of these notable people exhibit, I'd never expect to experience Depression or Anxiety. These people prove the "equally opportunity offender" theory to be true.[4]

Their impact and careers demonstrate an important fact about your journey: Your potential is not determined by the presence of Depression or Anxiety in your life.

In fact, I have a theory: I think the powerful byproduct of facing seasons of Depression and Anxiety might be *precisely* why these celebrities have been so successful. I truly believe that the very adversity you face can become your biggest advantage. If you're willing to find a *better* you, the process will inevitably shape you into a more positive, impactful person. You'll become someone who has an influential mix of *pinpointed intentionality, emotional resilience, steady perseverance,* and *life-giving empathy*.

Of course, we won't all become professional athletes, chart-topping musicians, movie stars, or famous influencers. Trust me, if you ever catch me on the court and witness my jump shot, you'll know that I was not destined for the NBA. If you get the opportunity to see me dance to the award-winning song "Single Ladies," I'll make a complete fool of myself. And, as much as I might wish I were 6'4" and 260 lbs. of pure *Baywatch* muscle like "The Rock," my genes screwed me on that one. But the truth is, we all have a specific niche to occupy on this earth.

I don't know where you are in life or what compelled you to pick up this book. But I can promise you this; your epic story has just begun. If you choose to approach this battle correctly, then fighting this season of Depression and Anxiety will lead to finding a *better* version of yourself—destined to thrive in your own, individual calling.

In fact, if there's one thing I know to be true, it's that *pain is never wasted*. It can be difficult to believe that during a storm, but it's the truth!

And here's another compelling truth:

When you expose a struggle, it loses its power.

So, shall we?

Let's break down Depression and Anxiety.

DEFINING DEPRESSION

· I N   A   R E A L   W A Y ·

The most logical place to start when discussing Depression is to define it. We need to know what we're up against...

Merriam Webster's Dictionary offers this definition:

> ➢ **DEPRESSION**: (1) a state of feeling sad (2) a *mood disorder* marked especially by sadness, inactivity, difficulty in thinking and concentration, a significant increase or decrease in appetite and time spent sleeping, feelings of dejection and hopelessness, and sometimes suicidal tendencies.[1]

I always start by defining a word when I need to get more context, but in the case of Depression, the traditional definition is too sterile. That's part of the problem. None of us (no matter how terrible we may feel) want to label ourselves as having a "mood disorder."

Just imagine seeing a Tinder profile like this:

I'm not on Tinder, but I'm pretty sure this bio would lead to plenty of left swipes!

In today's culture, we're encouraged to present our lives through the lens of a filter. In a world flooded with perfect Instagram posts, there's a hesitancy to show anything other than our edited best. Seemingly everyone is living a great life: energized, stress-free, and deliberately walking with passion and purpose. Therefore, labeling how we feel as a "*mood disorder*" seems far from acceptable.

Even though Depression is common in our culture, it's oddly ambiguous. So, disregard the academic definition, and let me define what I think Depression is truly like...

DEPRESSION is a state when there's an increased weight to the questions and thoughts entering your mind. In fact, Depression is the opposite of carefree thinking. It's the combination of intense *negativity* and *self-loathing* fueled by the after-burn of *worry* and *doubt*.

DEPRESSION makes false, critical claims about who you are, relentlessly repeating them in your mind to the point that you actually start believing them.

DEPRESSION is when you have a full conversation with someone, and yet you can't remember what they've said because you were entirely *consumed* and *distracted* by negative thoughts.

DEPRESSION is not moving, because movement requires energy. Your body is not willing to exert the energy necessary to accomplish anything. Whether or not this strikes you in the morning when you first wake up, or during prolonged moments throughout the day, conjuring up motivation and checking things off the list seems to reach a new level of unattainability.

Merriam Webster says that **DEPRESSION** can cause an increase in time spent sleeping. However, for a person facing Depression, this is not the case because sleeping is enjoyable. It's not like sleeping in on a Sunday morning—Jack Johnson "Banana Pancakes" style. A person struggling with Depression sleeps because the discouraging and exhausting thoughts temporarily disappear, thus allowing a much-needed break amidst the battle.

DEPRESSION is when you feel markedly down, smack-dab in the middle of a fun activity. No one would assume that feelings of Depression would be present while you're at a live concert of your favorite band, or on a date with the love of your life, or after acing a job interview; but that's how Depression works. It picks the most inconvenient and inexplicable times to edge its way into your life with unwarranted permission. In my life, there have been moments where I thought to myself, "Why do I feel so off right now? Why do I feel so down? I should be happy because I'm (fill in the blank)." But, I just couldn't shake it.

DEPRESSION is the "fear of failure, but with no urge to be productive. It's wanting friends, but dreading talking with people. It's wanting to be alone, but not wanting to be lonely."[2]

DEPRESSION is the inability to believe that you'll ever feel happy again. It conjures up thoughts that can be hard to accurately describe, but they're usually rooted in inadequacy. It feels like you won't get any better, feel any happier, or be able to handle what's to come next in life. When you're struggling with this feeling, it seems as if it'll never end. While this is irrational, anyone who has faced Depression knows that it's a very real conclusion that comes to mind.

DEPRESSION can sneak up on you without warning. One moment (day, week, etc.) you're fine, and then almost out of the blue, you can find yourself slipping into depressive thought-patterns with no ability to pinpoint the exact time or place where it all began. Once again, you're "stuck," and caught off guard, trying to reorient yourself to regain peace and optimism.

And for the sake of breaking down all stereotypes, DEPRESSION is not only reserved for the image of a person who seems outwardly "sad." In fact, watch out Hollywood, because people who struggle with Depression or Anxiety are often some of the world's greatest actors. We can put on a face, acting like life is all-good on the surface, but we're fighting a battle on the inside.

Even on my hardest days facing Depression, you better believe that I'll be smiling, suited up with High-Top Converse, Jordan crew socks, comfy sweat shorts, and a Champion hoodie, at least attempting to take on the day with what my idea of swagger looks like. So maybe it's the Instagram famous model, the sorority president, the athlete with the "C" on their jersey, the people at the party "having the time of their lives," or the smartest kid in class who's received multiple Ivy League scholarship offers... all who could be struggling. Anyone could be facing Depression and Anxiety on the inside, while they fight to keep it together on the outside.

That's **DEPRESSION**.

I've felt each one of these descriptions of Depression powerfully play out in my life at one point or another.

If any of this describes how you (or a person you know) are feeling, then Depression could be why. It's not some disease that you contracted because you're weak. It's not a "disorder" that will define you for the rest of your life. And… it sure as hell won't be allowed to consume any more of your life by the time you finish this book and initiate a plan to *find better*.

Now on to Anxiety…

DEFINING ANXIETY

DEPRESSION'S
BEST FRIEND

When I think about defining Depression, I automatically think about its best friend and closest companion: Anxiety. Don't be fooled, Anxiety should never be downplayed. For that reason, I think it's only fair that since Depression got the spotlight in the last chapter, Anxiety should get its shot at stardom.

Like Depression, I feel that Anxiety's standard academic definition doesn't cut it. We need to fully understand what Anxiety feels like to overcome it...

Well-known radio host Charlamagne tha God defines "Anxiety" as having the thought of... "I'm bad. I'm not good enough. I'm not going to have everything I need in this world to be OK. And then we freak out. Bam. Anxiety."[1]

I love this description because Anxiety can be as simple as that. Once we start to overthink our life, something we've done, or our ability to handle a situation, then anxious thoughts take the wheel and drive us down a path of worry.

However, if we can't control worry in our life, then we can never step out to perform at the level we need to. Honestly, while most of us are equipped to be successful where we are right now, Anxiety will try to convince us of the opposite.

Let me define what I think Anxiety looks and feels like...

ANXIETY convinces you that a potential negative outcome is more likely to happen than anything positive. For example, it conjures up adverse future outcomes like losing your job, failing a class, messing up a performance, indefinitely remaining single, or never finding a rewarding career path, and then, it magnifies those worries to overpower any attempt of optimism.

ANXIETY is worrying about what others may think of you: how you look, talk, or act. It's being hyper-aware of everything that you could be negatively or embarrassingly judged for, when in reality, no one even cares! The time leading up to any interaction is more stressful than it should be as a result of obsessively worrying (a.k.a. social Anxiety). This is why public speaking may very well be one of the most Anxiety producing situations. You're putting yourself on a platform, exposed to the judgment and opinions of others.

Will people like what I have to say? Will I deliver the message clearly without messing up?

ANXIETY can also manifest through physical symptoms. Your body can react with a response as common as nervous sweating, shortness of breath, restless sleep, or a racing heart. More severe responses like panic attacks, hives, or even stomach ulcers can happen as well.

ANXIETY is experiencing a mixture of Eminem's famous "Lose Yourself" lyrics with the unsettled feeling you have before a first date. It often happens before something that shouldn't even be nerve-wracking, like asking a professor for help after class, or before a Jimmy John's job interview (which isn't usually considered a highly competitive business environment). You can thank my endless bank of anxious moments for these two golden examples... but the point is that **ANXIETY** isn't logical.

ANXIETY comes from a buildup of feelings. When you feel anxious, or worse, have a panic attack, it's because "your body can no longer mask or contain the emotional unrest that's happening inside."[2] The same thing causes social Anxiety. It's a buildup of nervous thoughts and feelings that get in the way of confidently interacting with others. What's so important to realize though, is that just because you have a feeling, doesn't mean it's the truth.

ANXIETY is overanalyzing that weird bump on the back of your throat that you swear has developed within the last week. After a vigorous WebMD search, you realize that it's just your tonsils; it turns out that we all have them. (Just another one of my proudest freak-out moments!)

ANXIETY is feeling like you don't have control over something. Maybe you feel that you don't have control over your weight, acne, finances, or relationships. Rarely are things entirely out of our control. Instead, our obsessed urgency and heightened awareness to see the desired change causes the Anxiety. Ironically, these fears hinder our ability to take any necessary steps forward to generate the change we desperately want to see.

And if Anxiety and Depression weren't already confusing enough, on the random days where I feel slightly depressed—even though I know that I'll never have a season as bad as the one of my past—I get anxious that I'm slipping back into that really heavy state. I know it's nearly impossible since who I am today is radically different than who I was then, but Anxiety still tries to convince me that I'm weak and susceptible to experiencing that season again. I call BS, **ANXIETY**.

As with Depression, all of these descriptions of Anxiety have been present in my life at one time or another.

Here's the thing though. You and I will face uncertainty throughout each step of life. That's just how it is! Similar to the three little dots that pop up on our iPhones when we're waiting for an unknown message response, the same mystery of what's to come next happens on a grander scale in life. However, our ability to manage anxious thoughts during these times of uncertainty will directly determine our ability to make it through them. That's why calming our anxieties is so important.

———————————

Now that we have a better picture of what Depression and Anxiety are truly like, let's start *making "moves"* to send them walking out the door.

Buh-Bye Anxiety.

Buh-Bye Depression.

MAKING MOVES

· A PLAN OF ACTION ·

Heading into the fifth grade, I was full of "confidence" because I was finally going to be at the top of the school. For many elementary schools, fifth grade is the final grade before moving on to middle school. As "Kings and Queens" of the school, fifth-graders walk into the building with an inflated-level of superiority.

Imagine a tiny Ben Champion waltzing into homeroom, rocking Justin Bieber-esque hair, an Old Navy t-shirt, and smelling of Speed Stick deodorant (because I'm a man now, duh). The truth is, I was so lame back then! But, everybody knows that being in fifth grade means playing the part of Top Dog.

Be cool Ben... be cool.

The first couple of weeks were typical; I'd walk into school, stuff my oversized jacket and roller backpack in my cubby, and head to homeroom. Like clockwork, the 8:05 a.m. school announcements would play through the room's speakers, echoing down the halls. After two weeks of suffering through the long, boring announcement routine, I started to notice something peculiar. When the announcements started, I'd look across the room to find my best friend, Parker, but he was nowhere to be found. Then, ever so quietly, he'd sneak back into class around 8:20 a.m., oh-so conveniently after the drawn-out announcements. Ms. Miller, our teacher, seemed to not even notice his reoccurring tardiness.

I asked him, "Dude! Where are you during the morning announcements?"

Parker proudly replied, "I'm part of the chess club. It runs past announcements, so I don't have to come to class right away. Ms. Miller knows, and she's totally cool with it!"

Slightly stunned, I replied, "So you're telling me that every day, you get to play board games before school... and ditch announcements?! That's sick! Hook me up... I want in!"

Forty-eight hours later, I was a noble member of the school's chess club. I had found a new hobby that also came with precious tardy immunity.

Double score!

Now if you've never played chess before, it's not the easiest of board games. There are numerous pieces that each have unique moves associated with them. For this reason, the game requires *deep concentration* and *deliberate strategizing.*

You're probably wondering, "What does chess have to do with Depression and Anxiety?" Let me explain. There are lots of struggling people who are facing Depression and/or Anxiety as their "opponent." And for one reason or another, they may be losing. One of the realities that we encounter with our personal battle is that it's rarely an easy fight. Depression and Anxiety are *complex, intertwined issues* that wrap themselves around our lives.

Don't take this next phrase lightly:

You must face Depression and Anxiety as if you were facing an opponent in *chess* rather than in *checkers.*

Chess is complicated and challenging. It requires players to make many unique moves.

Checkers is simple and easy. It only requires the use of one basic move.

If facing Depression and Anxiety were like playing checkers, then there'd be one move that if repeated enough would result in a calculated win. But this approach doesn't cut it for beating Depression and/or Anxiety. Don't half-heartedly fight your symptoms or approach healing from only one angle hoping that you'll win. I'm not saying Depression or Anxiety is a game. I'm merely using this analogy so that you can recognize the depth and difficulty that these struggles present in our lives.

––––––––––

After two months of attending chess club, we had our first chess tournament. I was amped and eager to get my first win by flexing my board game muscles. My first round was against a third-grade girl who couldn't have been taller than 4 feet.

I thought to myself, "I have this in the bag."

Unwavering, the girl sat down with her shoulders drawn back, making direct eye contact—staring me down with the eyes of a lion. Sheepishly, I kept my eyes on the board.

"Dang, she means business," I thought to myself. "Maybe she's better than I think."

The outcome?

Five minutes later, I was in checkmate with almost all of my pieces eliminated from the board.

So much for feeling like Top Dog!

––––––––––

The difference between my embarrassing tournament loss to a third grader, and my fight with Depression and Anxiety, is that in the much more important battle... I'm winning. I may not always feel 100%, and there are days when the opponent makes some pretty strong moves against me. But, I have my strategy, and I'm continually *making moves*. Therefore, I will ultimately continue to be the victor.

Each of the following chapters in this book discuss crucial **"moves"** (an angle, an area, a topic) you should explore going forward. When you've had enough—and sometimes it can take a while to get to that point—you must go at Depression and Anxiety with every swift, strategic **"move"** you've got.

PART II

THE MIND

VANILLA OR CHOCOLATE

THOUGHT MANAGEMENT

Have you ever had ice cream from one of those industrial-sized soft serve machines? They're a gift to mankind. To the inventor of soft serve: Thank you for changing the dessert game forever.

With the most basic models, there are three options offered: vanilla, chocolate, and, (if you know what's up) a swirl of both. Most of us have had the pleasure to step up, armed with a cone in our hand, and pull the lever to begin filling it up with soft serve goodness. Usually, the machine works fine, slowly dispensing the ice cream as we wait impatiently, piling up our cones with as much ice cream as possible.

However, have you ever encountered what happens when things don't go as planned? The machine freaks out. A rumbling sound emerges from inside the beast, and the lever disengages. The soft serve flows out of the machine uncontrollably.

Initial joy becomes *immediate panic!* Ice cream is everywhere, and the machine has no intention of stopping. Your cone has no room left, and you stand there in shock as the mess unfolds right in front of you!

Whether we realize it or not, when we're depressed or anxious, our thoughts are like a rogue soft serve machine, uncontrollably flowing into our mind at a frightening rate. It may start with a single thought, but then that triggers more and more thoughts, becoming a mess of unstoppable *insecurity*, *worry*, and *discouragement* overflowing in our mind.

When we're feeling depressed or anxious, we don't have control over our thoughts. This is why managing our thoughts is the key to managing our emotions.

Let me emphasize this because this concept is so important...

Thought Management = Emotional Management

Have you ever felt anxious or depressed while also feeling thoughts that were calm and in control? Of course not! It's not possible. When we're feeling that way, our minds are inevitably racing. While we may seem externally present, we often have unrelenting, negative thoughts "boomeranging" around in our mind.

So how can we start to fight back and shift our mind in a better direction?

1. RECOGNIZE NEGATIVE THOUGHTS

It all begins with fostering self-awareness. This means grabbing ahold of negative thoughts by recognizing how false, dramatic, or detrimental they are. You must develop the ability to read how you're feeling in a certain moment, and then translate that feedback into a game plan for modification. The more you start intentionally addressing Depression and Anxiety, the better you'll get at sensing when your thoughts are moving in the wrong direction.

Self-awareness is like proactively watching out for a "DEAD END" sign at the beginning of a road. It's realizing that if you keep thinking a certain way, the outcome won't be where you want to end up. With strong self-awareness comes the ability to see the sign and make a decision to turn back and hop on the interstate—headed in a better direction.

One of the many traps we fall into when we're struggling with Depression or Anxiety is stating "absolute phrases" over our current season of life. Absolute phrases use words like "always," "never," "everyone," etc. They are words that claim something is 100% correct or bound to happen.[1] A negative absolute phrase is a "DEAD END" road just waiting to be traveled on.

Initially, I wasn't aware that this was something I was doing often. Once I became aware of these thought-patterns, I recognized how unreasonable it was for me to think this way about my life.

Here are some common examples of absolute phrases that people say:

- "I will NEVER find a person who wants to date me."
- "I will ALWAYS struggle with my weight."
- "I fail at EVERYTHING I try."
- "ALL of my options suck."
- "I will DEFINITELY not get this job."
- "I CANNOT become a morning person." (Still working on this one myself)
- "I'm gonna feel like this FOREVER. It's just who I am."

Once I recognized that I was boxing myself in by thinking in absolutes, I was able to disqualify the extremes that I was placing over my life. If you're thinking in absolutes, your brain is becoming hardwired to not expect anything other than the negative outcome you've convinced yourself will inevitably happen. There's rarely a situation in life that's worthy of absolute phrasing, no matter how challenging or discouraging it may feel in the moment. I can only think of two absolute phrases that I can wholeheartedly backup: I will NEVER get tired of watching *The Office*, and NOTHING is better than Nutella!

In my life, I've worked hard to exercise more self-awareness so I can spot when my thoughts are starting to head in the wrong direction. Whether it's an absolute phrase or simply unchecked, negative thoughts, I recognize the thought-pattern and then work to pivot in a better direction.

Take a step back when you start feeling anxious or depressed and try to pinpoint the main thought causing those feelings. Challenge yourself by asking: *Why am I having this thought? Why do I feel this way? Is there an unrealistic expectation I'm placing upon myself? Am I afraid of something in the future that may not even happen?*

2. REPLACE NEGATIVE THOUGHTS

The next step is to strive to replace the negative thought or thought-patterns. Take what you might naturally be thinking about and consciously choose to think about something inversely positive. Both negative and positive thinking soak up brainpower, so you might as well focus energy on turning things around.

Granted, this is one of the hardest things to do when you're feeling depressed or anxious. It's why we roll our eyes when people say, "Just think happier thoughts." Many of us can agree that thinking negatively sometimes feels like second nature. It's like our brain tries to conjure up stress, worry, or dissatisfaction before we even have a chance to impartially evaluate a situation. If someone says to us, "Just snap out of it!" We know that a reversal just doesn't work like that. It may take some time for us to get out of the deep groove we've settled in; however, *it's possible.* You *must* learn how to redirect your thoughts, even if it feels like an uphill battle.

I once heard a phrase from a speaker named Levi Lusko who said, "You can't live a positive life if you have negative thoughts." It's a basic remark; yet when I heard it, it shook me. All of a sudden, the truth of his words clicked for me. I realized, "It doesn't matter how great of a life I hope to have, the direction of my thoughts will determine the direction of my life."

A while ago, I listened to a podcast interview between Lewis Howes and a champion Mixed Martial Arts (MMA) fighter, Mike Chandler.[2] Lewis, the host, was asking Mike some questions about his daily habits as a successful athlete, wondering what his approach was to stay on top as a fighter and influencer. More specifically, Lewis asked him, "What are you thinking right before a fight?"

Mike said:

"I stop listening to myself... and start speaking over myself. If I just sit there in silence and listen to myself, I hear things that aren't even rational. The more you're talking to yourself, the less you can hear yourself." (To clarify, he didn't necessarily mean an audible conversation out loud, but an inner conversation with yourself.)

Instead, he starts telling himself: "I can do this. I've worked hard to get here. I'm just as ready and deserving as my opponent."

You couldn't pay me enough money to fight MMA, but I do know that his approach is precisely what we all must do to conquer the lies that enter our heads. I've taken the same practice into my day-to-day inner conversations by making sure I'm telling myself the truth about my situation and capabilities. Instead of listening to the endless lineup of "what ifs," "not enoughs," and "cannots" that show up regularly, I protect my mind by keeping lies from distorting my worth.

Don't mistake this advice as a claim that simply stating positive one-liners will dramatically change your life. There's a misconception in some self-help content that stating positive claims/demands and sending them out into the Universe will cause amazing change to manifest in one's life. While this may not be totally false, there's a right and wrong approach to this concept.

Here's what I mean:

WRONG: "I will be successful!"

RIGHT: "I'm capable of working hard, and I've done it before. I know that if I can produce quality work and learn from my mistakes, then I'll develop a successful career I'm proud of."

WRONG: "I will be wealthy!"

RIGHT: "I know that becoming wealthy starts with having good financial habits. So... I'm going to pay off any debt I have by saving more than I spend. I'm going to pursue job opportunities that show promising growth, and I'm going to practice being content with where I am now financially. If I start earning additional money, it'll be the icing on the cake."

WRONG: "I will be happy!"

RIGHT: "I want to be happier today than I was yesterday. Even though I know life has its ups and downs, my level of gratitude for this season of life is a daily choice. So, I'm going to be grateful for the little things like a hot shower, a roof over my head, and bagels (thank God for bagels!). However, I also know that I'm happier when I take the time to create a simple to-do list and actually do it, so I'll start there. I know that I'm happier when I limit my time on social media, so I'm logging off for the day. And on top of that, I'm going to grab coffee with a friend to catch up, knowing that I'll feel better after that as well."

See the major difference between each of those examples? Stating blanket-like lottery requests off into the Universe isn't the positive thinking I'm talking about. I'm talking about being realistic and deliberate about your daily approach to positive thinking. This creates the perfect combination of objectives and optimism, producing positive steps to work yourself out of negative thought-patterns.

Kicking it up a notch, replacing negative thoughts requires action. When we sit in our heavy thoughts, they multiply and magnify—leading to an overwhelming mental state that would hinder anyone.

So, in addition to speaking rationally and positively about myself and my life, I have a list of action-oriented approaches I take to replace and redirect negative thoughts:

Talk It Out

- Sometimes the best solution is having someone else look at your situation from the outside and remind you why things are more manageable than they seem.

Find A Fresh Zip Code

- If you've been stuck inside all day, or hunkered down studying for hours, pick up your things and find a new location. It's amazing how much a change of scenery can change our state-of-mind.

Change Your Pace

- Our bodies respond positively to movement—it clears our heads. We were meant to live healthy, active lives; the state of our minds depend on that vital foundation, so kick up your pace a notch or two.

Live To Serve

- Isolation feeds Depression. When we serve, we take the focus off of ourselves and on to helping someone else.

Get'cha Hands Dirty

- Even though it feels more natural to remain idle when we're struggling with Depression or Anxiety, inactivity perpetuates these feelings. When I came back struggling from college, I chose to find a summer job. It wasn't anything super   challenging.   But having somewhere to be each day was better than having to manage large chunks of open time.

Text It Out

- I don't journal my thoughts down with pen and paper (although you can), but I'll whip out my Notes app when I need to clear my head. I'll text out what I'm feeling, and then try to challenge myself as to *why*. If I have a realization or creative thought, I'll type it out to make sure I can acknowledge it later.

Avoid "Struggle Amnesia"

- We can easily forget the problems in our past that we've made it through. This is called "struggle amnesia." Once we conquer a problem, it's on to the next problem that we feel is insurmountable. Remember an event from your past that you were able to overcome, and approach your current challenge through the lens of that past success. *I made it through "_____," so I'll make it through "_____."*

Never Stop Learning

- In this day and age of digital expansion, we have more access to positive messages than ever — take advantage of that. Whether you choose to listen to a podcast, sermon, or watch meaningful YouTube videos, find speakers and influencers that you connect with. Find the speakers that are authentic and truthful about life. Let their advice penetrate any negative perspectives.

Use Distraction In Moderation

- Sometimes the best remedy for stopping negative thoughts is finding a distraction. Use distraction (in moderation) like listening to music, watching/playing digital content, or reading to derail negative thought-patterns (S/O to Spotify's "Discover Weekly" and late-night *SportsCenter*).

Once we're able to *recognize* and *replace* the thoughts in our head, the final piece to better thought management is *reinforcing* the changes we've made.

3. REINFORCE POSITIVE THOUGHTS

What are you telling yourself on repeat?

...because, how you speak to yourself determines your mental and emotional posture.

Our brains are full of what scientists call "neural pathways." Whenever we react a certain way or think a certain thought, a pathway is created or reinforced. Over time, the pathways become more and more ingrained into the makeup of our brains as they're increasingly used. Neurologists have monitored participants' neural reactions in real-time with MRI machines to see what causes our brains to "light up." They ultimately found that "we strengthen whichever neural pathways we use most often." This is why, after a long period of depressed or anxious thinking, it seems like second nature to continue in the same way.

However, scientists have also found that "neural pathways of the brain change over time — the brain is dynamic, not fixed."[3] They call this "neuroplasticity." What's so encouraging about this discovery is that we can change negative neural pathways, create new ones, and rewire our brain to think more positively. Compare this process to muscle memory. Think of how dunking becomes second nature for professional basketball players, or how dancers can memorize a routine through repetition. In the same way, we can reinforce better reactions to triggers such as stress, uncertainty, social interaction, or self-judgment through reinforcing better thought-patterns.

Managing your thoughts as a person who's prone to Depression or Anxiety is like potty training a dog. You're training your thoughts by rewiring your current thought tendencies. You have to keep reinforcing the new pathways until it becomes second nature to think the new and improved thought on a regular basis. Now, when a negative thought pops into my head, similar to a puppy that's about to pee inside on my swanky, twenty-dollar IKEA rug, I say, "Whoaaaaa...... Nope! Hold up. Not gonna happen!" I know the outcome of this thought-pattern if I let it go unchecked... so I won't let it!

What I've just laid out is not meant to be merely "RAH! RAH!" advice, unfairly demanding that you simply "pick yourself up by the bootstraps" and immediately have positive thoughts in a matter of minutes. There's likely a fuel behind the flame of your thoughts. Behind every negative thought is a deeper feeling which stands in the background pressing that thought forward. These thoughts can be prompted by feelings of fear, anger, narcissism, scarcity, insecurity, or pain:

- Maybe you've been hurt by a friend or family member.
- Maybe you're worn out from trying to be liked.
- Maybe it's been forever since you've appreciated yourself.
- Maybe the uncertainty of what's to come keeps your thoughts continually spinning.

- Maybe your past failures are unfairly driving future expectations.

Whatever the case, it's possible to have a better thought life. Although, no doubt, you have your work cut out for you.

Wrapping all of this up, what would this chapter be without the stereotypical "self-help book" motivational alliteration?

So here ya go…
The 3 R's of thought management:
1) **Recognize.**
2) **Replace.**
3) **Reinforce.**

In time, you'll find a better version of yourself. This version will be more in charge of your thoughts and will know how to get out of a valley if you wander into one.

That's what I call good thought management.

That's what I call… *Better.*

TAKEAWAYS

- Learning how to manage thoughts takes self-awareness and intentionality. *Thought Management = Emotional Management.*
- You control the attention and direction that you assign to every thought.
- Follow the 3R's: (1) Recognize negative thoughts, (2) Replace negative thoughts with positive ones, and (3) Reinforce the positive thoughts.

PACKAGING PERFECTION

· SOCIAL MEDIA ·

During the summer of my eighth-grade year, my family took a three-week trip to Europe. My dad, who's a teacher and avid explorer, planned for our family to visit as many cities as possible. We were set to sleep in Europe's most luxurious one-star hostels and travel with only the essentials shoved into backpacks.

One of the most unforgettable nights of the trip happened in Paris. We arrived in the city with a mere 24 hours to see all that it had to offer before hurriedly traveling to the next place.

The day was spent visiting multiple attractions like the Louvre and the Arc de Triomphe. By dinnertime, we were exhausted! My sister and I begged to end the day early and head back to our hostel for some extra rest, but my dad was determined to make sure we saw one more monument... the Eiffel Tower.

We took the train for a couple of miles across the city to make it to the tower before it closed. I have to say, once we got there, I was blown away. The tower itself is magnificent, standing over a thousand feet tall![1] The view of Paris at night looking out from the top of the tower is one of sparkling store-front lights and glowing traffic. It's something I'll never forget. But the view was not the only thing that I'll never forget. The night had just begun!

We left the tower around 11:00 p.m. and hopped on the train headed back toward our hostel. The train was tightly packed since it was one of the last of the night. Two exits into our ride, the train completely stopped. Slight panic spread throughout the train car as people wondered if this was going to be more than just a brief inconvenience. Five minutes later, people really started to get anxious. Then, to make matters worse, all of the power went off: the air conditioning, the lights, all of it. Everyone on the Métro started losing it!

People attempted to shift around, but there was nowhere to go. They were stepping on toes and exchanging angry words with one another. My dad reassured us that the train would start back up at any minute and that we'd all be okay. I'd like to say that I believed him, but my mind was stuck on the passengers that were uncomfortably leaning up against me, and the seemingly depleting air around me. A man behind me had his sweaty back pressed up against mine as if we were two squished-together Haribo gummy bears. Coming from somebody who should be sponsored by Purell, this was my breaking point. I started to freak out! Claustrophobic and worried, my heart was pounding, my breathing was erratic, and my mind was racing.

Another miserable fifteen minutes went by before the train finally lurched forward. We slowly rolled to the next stop about a quarter-mile up the track. Once there, the doors were pried open, and everyone was let out. An announcement stated that there'd be no more stops for the night. The good news was that we were safely off the train from hell. The bad news was that we were still a long way from our hostel. We thought the walk back was doable, so we set out from there.

We quickly realized that even with our memory of exploring the city earlier, we weren't quite sure how to get back at night. We were tired and lost, walking in a foreign city late at night (pre-smartphones). It was awful!

We started to pinball our way up through the city, gradually finding our way back. After three hours and many sketchy alleys later, we finally arrived at our hostel. What's funny though, is that we only have a couple of family photos of that day spent in Paris; a photo taken at the Arc de Triomphe and another at the Eiffel tower. Our pictures of that leg of the trip fail to show all of the chaotic, stressful details of that night.

Just like our photo prints of Paris, social media leaves out the real, unglamorous details of life. Most posts on social media don't show the whole picture (pun intended). Think about it! If Instagram was a thing back then, my "Paris post" would have been of the four of us happily smiling atop the Eiffel Tower. The post would have left out the low points of the day, like the fact that I had a public panic attack on the train. Or, that my family was irritated and exhausted as we wandered back to our hostel. From an outsider's perspective, no one would have known otherwise.

There've been times in the past where I've posted content of an "awesome" event, or workout, or outing, and yet, in reality, my day was quite awful. There've been mornings where I was stuck in worried and depressed thoughts, but my social presence didn't reflect those insecurities. I still proceeded to post a story showing a modern coffee shop where I diligently "worked on a new project." The story post made it look like I was enjoying a fancy iced beverage while also being inspired and productive. In reality, I had been procrastinating on my project and imprisoned by pessimistic thoughts. This is the common problem with social media; we often present only precisely filtered moments.

Now, I'm not calling everyone out! You may be open and organic with your posts. You may not even use social media at all *#BlessUp*. But for the majority of profiles, consistently presenting our ideal self is the norm.

How does this relate to Depression and Anxiety?

We're inundated with posts of happy, beautiful people across all social media platforms. If we feel depressed or anxious, and yet see endless content of our peers having "constant" fun, looking unbelievably attractive, and appearing uber-successful, we can quickly jump to the conclusion that we're the only person struggling.

Then, shame emerges, generated by the feeling that we're struggling and no one else is. Who wants to feel like the broken vessel, while everyone else seemingly steams ahead in the right direction? It's likely a partial reason for the rapidly increasing suicide rate, especially in high school (70% increase within 10-17 year-olds from '06 to '16).[2] Young adults feel more insecure and lonelier than ever because of pitting themselves up against flawless social media facades. Even digital industry leaders have commented on this negative byproduct of social platforms. Steve Bartlett, CEO of Social Chain, a global social media agency, stated, "Social media has made perfect look normal."[3] It could be said that social media is in the business of *#PackagingPerfection*.

This awareness about social media isn't a breakthrough discovery anymore and shouldn't be a new realization for us.

Five years ago, the questions about social media were these:

- Does social media promote unrealistic standards?
- Does social media provoke comparison?
- Does social media enable close connection, or does it hinder it?
- Is social media addictive?
- Is social media a trigger leading to increased feelings of Anxiety and Depression?

We questioned whether Facebook, Instagram, YouTube, Snapchat, Twitter, etc. were going to radically change our mood, behaviors, and outlook. But, the question of whether or not social media affects our lives is no longer relevant. We know it does!

These are the predictable outcomes—good and bad—that we run into when we scroll through our feeds:

You and I know… that social media can be a good form of entertainment. But, we also know it can easily distract us from being productive, e.g., getting trapped in the endless stream of Facebook content or watching random YouTube videos.

Sometimes… we look at influencers with hundreds of thousands of followers, and their body, message, or business genuinely inspires us. However, other times we look at their pages and leave feeling unattractive and insignificant.

Often… we use social media to stay up to date and informed. Yet unfortunately, we also confront unfavorable political debates, false news, and derogatory content when we log on.

For the most part… we view our friends' stories and genuinely enjoy watching their content. But other times, we get caught up in analyzing what others are doing. We think: *What am I missing out on? They look like they are having the time of their life… must be nice!*

We know that… there are times when we post a special moment like spending time with friends and family, or a personal achievement like a graduation post, and we actually do feel valued and loved. We feel like that moment is worthy of being shared.

However, we all experience inevitable unglamorous and mundane moments each day too—these moments are rarely revealed to our social media circles.

The majority of us have... taken a picture we really like. But, we've also taken pictures and immediately categorized them as "non-postable," critically disqualifying each one because of minor flaws.

And finally, most of us have at one point or another... logged on to connect with someone by using social media as a tool to catch up. However, we've also seen a post from an ex, an estranged family member, or a friend we've lost a connection with, leaving us to deal with a mixed bag of emotions.

I once heard this phrase: "Social media is a full-contact sport." It's so true! You have to have a game plan for your approach. You have to be prepared. You have to have your head up, conscious of how social media is affecting your confidence and outlook. We can't stay glued to social media and not expect to be altered in some way. This all sounds bleak, but it's not meant to discourage you! Rather, it's a reminder to act with self-awareness when getting on social media.

The new, relevant question we should be asking is: *How can we make sure social media is a positive part of our life instead of a negative one?*

A simple question, but the implications and answers are serious.

To make social media a positive part of your life, start by setting up healthy boundaries around the amount of time and attention you give each platform.

If you're like me, I mindlessly check social media for no other reason than out of habit and boredom. I swipe open my phone and click on Instagram almost automatically. It happens all the time! However, I've found that completely logging off helps break this habit. This forces me to briefly pause and re-enter my login information every time I want to get back on. This mini-hurdle is enough for me to question, *Why am I logging on?* If I realize that I've opened the app for no important reason, I close it and get back to living. Try it out! This extra step will cause you to think twice.

Other helpful "boundary setting" practices include:

- Deleting the apps that aren't necessary for your personal growth. (I deleted both Twitter and Snapchat for this reason.)
- Picking one day a week to disconnect from social media. You can even join forces with a friend to support each other.

- Utilizing the "Screen Time" feature pre-programmed on newer devices to set limits on your content consumption.
- Asking a friend or family member to set a new password for your social media accounts. This way you have to go through them to log on. (I did this for a month and got so much done!)

Ask yourself:
- How much time do I spend on social media? Is it the first thing I check when I get up in the morning, or the last thing I do before I fall asleep?
- Do the influencers I follow build me up? Or, do their accounts just add to the clutter of content I see?
- Am I confident in being myself? Or, do I place too much value on the likes and comments my posts receive?

Depending on your answers to these questions, you may find that setting boundaries could be the best thing for you.

In fact, a "boundary setting" movement is emerging with our generation. In the last year, the ORIGIN Market Research Group found that "34% of

Generation Z social media users have quit one or more platforms entirely, while a full 64% have taken at least a temporary break."[4]

Every time I've chosen to disconnect from social media, I've felt markedly better. I've had periods ranging from one week to four months where I've left an app, temporarily deleting it, challenging myself to give it a break. What's crazy is that not once have I missed my feeds. Admittedly, I'm not to the point of complete detachment, but I've become a fan of these cyclical breaks, resetting my perspective and investing energy in my true in-person relationships. Give it a try, and see for yourself the positive impact this change can have on your life.

———————

The scary truth about social media is that it can edit, filter, and erase all of the authenticity from our lives. Nothing in history has challenged our individual authenticity as much as social media.

➤ **AUTHENTIC:** true to oneself, genuine[5]
Synonyms: actual, original, the real thing

When you and I are authentic, a heavy weight is taken off our shoulders to be something we're not. We're content with who we are—imperfections and all. We connect with people because they feel comfortable with us; not because of the way we look or what we've accomplished. People naturally want to be around us because of the inner peace we give off. They can sense this, and they admire it. This is because authenticity is…

Refreshing. Empowering. Contagious.

We have to chase authenticity every day, continually working to become the original, one-of-a-kind version of ourselves that positively impacts those around us. We can't let unchecked social media skew our self-worth or our innate human value. We can't let it disrupt the authenticity of our life or the peace of our soul…

All this to say: *Disconnect* and *reset.*

Reset your priorities.

Reset your mindset.

Reset your focus…

Reset your ~~social~~ soul.

TAKEAWAYS

- Realize that social media presents a highlight reel of people's lives. Never compare your day-to-day to someone else's post-to-post.
- Set clear boundaries with social media to maintain a healthy mindset.
- Strive to live an authentic life by caring less about what you see or post on social media and more about embracing the originality of yourself.

THE PRESSURE IS GOOD FOR YOU
A PERSPECTIVE ON SUCCESS

Does any of this sound familiar?

"Let's GOOO!!! What are you doing?!
Get up!   Get going!   Get driven!

If you're not **WORKING HARDER** than the
person next to you, then you're gonna get
passed up!

There are **24 HOURS** a day. How many hours
are you **HUSTLING** and **GRINDING?** Every hour
should be spent getting **SMARTER**, **WEALTHIER**,
and **CLOSER**. Closer to the destination.
Can you see it?

It's called success, and it ain't gonna come easy.

This is what's called, "Hustle Culture." It's become a popular mainstream message touted by celebrity entrepreneurs and influencers that encourages exhaustive efforts to become more well-known and successful.[1]

There's a perfect visual example of this perspective inside a bar downtown. When I drive by it, I see bright, neon signs flashing from inside the building. Hanging from the walls, there are three or four of these large, luminous signs, all displaying different motivational quotes. One sign always catches my eye. Maybe, it's because the sign is the biggest one. Perhaps, it's because it faces out toward the street. But most likely, it's because of what it says. In beaming, yellow letters,

"THE PRESSURE IS GOOD FOR YOU"

is boldly stated, projecting light through the window and casting onto the street.

I'm not going to lie. Every once in a while, this kind of talk can get me pumped up. With a strong cup of coffee and a little bit of Kendrick in the background, I can vibe with a *hustle mentality*. Yet at the same time, these messages can be unsettling, promoting the wrong approach to living a better life. For that reason, I read and repeat the words in my head and question if I really agree with the sign's statement.

Here's the thing... I believe that pressure in our lives is good to a certain point. Pressure is an inevitable aspect of life—increasing as we grow up. However, in our current pressure-filled culture, *success* and *recognition* have become widespread expectations placed upon us. A research-based poll was conducted by Inc.com to measure the pressure variances between younger and older generations. "It turns out Millennials do feel more pressure." The poll found that "67% of them said they felt 'extreme' pressure to succeed, compared to 40% of Gen Xers and 23% of Boomers."[2] If one thought that the pressure to be successful, attractive, and known was prevalent for people a decade ago, then multiply that level of pressure tenfold to grasp what we now feel on a daily basis.

In our current culture, we're experiencing increased pressure in two forms: *spoken* and *unspoken*.

SPOKEN PRESSURE is exactly what I described above. It's the audible claims that celebrity entrepreneurs, CEO's, and influencers label as success. It's the constant verbal and visual message presented that, as a culture, we need to accomplish more to be successful and happy in life.

UNSPOKEN PRESSURE is that which we internally place on ourselves. It develops from a combination of our own expectations and comparison to others. It's the standards we've put upon ourselves to perform at a certain level, to look a certain way, or to live a certain life. Whether this pressure is developed consciously or unconsciously, it can easily be distorted to unhealthy levels.

The perfect example of this is the increased pressure to be attractive. No one is really talking about its prevalence, but we can feel it when we scroll through Instagram. It's on another level right now! Don't misunderstand me. I'm not against anyone rockin' what they've got (shout-out portrait mode), but I do know that collectively, there must be many people who feel like they don't measure up to the influencer beauty benchmark.

There's unspoken pressure for men to have a shredded physique and rep brand name apparel, paired with a Zac Efron-like profile (no offense man). Simultaneously, there's unspoken pressure for women to be "proportionate" in all the right areas—looking stunning while at the gym, the beach, or at a party (basically looking perfect all the time). If left unchecked, this unhealthy pressure drives us to reach for more and more superficial gains and shallow social status. This is why so many young adults' posts are merely aimed to showcase the ability to look good.

The exceedingly high pressure to be perfect drags us down, opening the door for Depression and Anxiety.

———————

Since part of Depression and Anxiety is usually a lack of self-confidence, these two forms of pressure can weigh heavily on our mental state. In less than five minutes, you and I can find over a hundred people on social media with more likes and followers than us. There are limitless athletes, musicians, models, actors, and business tycoons who are seemingly living life on a grander level. If we're not careful, we fall into a "comparison trap," comparing our significance to an endless stream of people who *deceivingly* seem "more significant."

Here's the bottom line: These two forms of pressure are here to stay. So, our ability to handle them in regard to our appearance and performance may be one of the biggest keys to guarding our mental health.

These four suggestions can help you manage success-based pressure:

1. WHAT'S YOUR NATURAL TENDENCY?

First, start by examining your personality. Do you have a natural tendency to overemphasize the desire to be successful? Some people feel an inordinate amount of pressure to achieve and receive recognition, while others sit back, avoiding the spotlight. Some people naturally yell, "SHOTGUN!" while others happily claim, "back-seat middle."[3] Initiating self-awareness in this area can help you figure out which type of person you are.

2. WHAT'S YOUR DEFINITION OF SUCCESS?

Second, try precisely formulating your own beliefs on success. Define what success looks like for you, not what success looks like for influencer #1 or business guru #2. What are the main things you want to achieve, that if accomplished, would add up to a pretty darn successful life?

For example, as much as I want to be successful in my career, I also want to be a great dad. One of my future determinants of success will be raising a healthy, connected family. So, if the crazy rich CEO says that success is all about making more sales and merging large companies, although as a result, he or she doesn't spend enough quality time with their family, then maybe our view of success is different. If I couldn't have them both, I'd feel more successful being a rock-solid dad than a work-focused CEO.

Another example is that I'd rather take time off to travel than make more money. If it came down to either working fifty out of the fifty-two weeks a year to make an additional profit, or working forty-seven out of the fifty-two weeks, but having more time to travel, then I'd pick the latter. In my opinion, having five weeks off to travel, flying economy, taking uberPOOL rides, turning my phone off, and dining at cheap hole-in-the-wall restaurants is worth a lower salary. That beats only having a couple of weeks off, flying business class, answering endless work emails, eating overpriced Filet Mignon, and staying in four-star hotel rooms that have a Hershey's chocolate waiting for you on the pillow. Wait… I take back the Hershey's thing. I still want that!

So, define what success looks like for you, and then allocate the right amount of motivation and discipline to accomplish it.

3. WHAT'S YOUR LANE?

Next, you have to accurately manage the concept of "being known." How important is pursuing a life aimed at receiving a "blue checkmark?"

I've been noticing a crazy phenomenon that I like to call the "Public Figure Muffin Shop Dilemma." You may be wondering, "What the heck is that?" Let me explain. With a couple of clicks, anyone can label their Instagram or Facebook profile as "Public Figure." Have you seen it? Many accounts, regardless of the number of followers, are labeled as a "Public Figure." Now listen, I'm all for people like Oprah, Justin Timberlake, or Michael Jordan being rightly regarded as Public Figures. But, when you see a muffin shop owner labeled as a public figure... well, you get my point. To earn that honor, they'd better sell some fire muffins!

I'm talkin':
- Muffins that are zero-calorie
- Muffins that give the power of flight
- Muffins that bring world peace

Now those are some Public Figure worthy muffins! #InstaFamous

While the concept of verified accounts and influencers is still a newer social measure, the cause behind this "Public Figure Dilemma" is likely our ever-growing human desire to be socially significant (a.k.a. more pressure). It's an interesting time in which to live: balancing a genuine desire to make the world better, and at the same time having a healthy perspective on aspirations to be recognized and significant. I can tell you what I've decided is the best approach to handle our recognition-driven culture: To live with daily peace and purpose, and at the same time to excel in a given capacity, you have to find your lane. What are you gifted in, most passionate about, and believe you can use to positively impact people? Figure out your message, define your mission, and then maximize your lane. For example:

Maybe you're an aspiring model; it's your passion. Don't just model for the sake of getting more followers; do it for something more substantial. Maybe you have the mission to emotionally impact people through visual art, but also, to stir movement in that industry by being on the forefront of trends. You decide to partner your modeling platform with a philanthropy outreach so that as one grows, so does the other. WATCH OUT … now that's a lane.

Or maybe you're a photographer. Don't just take pictures to get likes. Dig deeper. Maybe you're on a mission to capture the connection between couples. You know the joy they'll receive from the prints, but you also know that amidst a *swipe right culture*, solid relationships should be treasured. You want to showcase that. NOW WE'RE TALKIN'… that's a lane.

Let's say that you're an up-and-coming musician. You love making music because of the joy it brings you. Don't just produce music for more downloads. Your mission could be to produce music in such a way that you're able to create a similar reaction of connection and joy in every listener. NOW HOW 'BOUT THAT... that's a lane.

Maybe you're a police officer, teacher, nurse, accountant, barista, intern, etc. Instead of just working for a paycheck, your lane becomes passionately showing up every day to make those around you feel valued through what you do. You work to set-up others for success, i.e., creating a safe community, fostering a passion for learning in students, getting a sick patient to smile, helping to grow a start-up, making the world's best caramel macchiato, or impressing a boss who's looking to promote (see what I did there). LOOK OUT... each of those are a lane.

Maybe you're wondering what my lane is?

I want to expose Depression and Anxiety in such a way that young adults facing either can experience breakthrough and *find better*. I want to talk about Depression and Anxiety through a modern, understandable lens; not overly academic or medical—just normal. I want to be so authentic and open about my struggles that others don't feel alone. I want to be able to connect and counsel with people in any setting: one-on-one, group discussion, streaming, written word, you name it. And if talking about Depression and Anxiety were ever seen as cool and relatable (not some stigma), then

FINDING BETTER would be the closest thing to it. BANG… that's my lane.

Our generation has to stop trying to be known just to be *known*. Find your lane and create more *impact*…

Open your notes app (or pen and paper) and start brainstorming. Even if you're not doing what you ultimately dream of doing, consider the impact you could have right here, right now. Clarify your current lane and define a mission to maximize this season.

Start by asking yourself:
- Am I on a path to make someone or something better?
- Why do I show up every day to work, school, sports, etc.? *(There's always a better answer than "just because" or "to make more money." If you really don't have a meaningful answer, then maybe it's time to pivot.)*

Going further, fill out this sentence:

I want to help and impact (*insert a group of people, company, or industry*) by using my (*insert a skill, passion, or attitude*) so that they/it can (*insert a positive objective or outcome*).

4. HOW DO YOU MANAGE EVERYDAY PRESSURE?

Finally, you have to put systems in place to regulate the pressure you encounter on a daily basis.

For the longest time, I never felt like I was ever doing enough. Even if I had a productive day, there was a gnawing after-thought begging the question, *What else could I have done?* The best solution I've found to help minimize the pressure to be successful is quite simple. I now write out a "sticky note success list." Each night, I make a list of four to five things that I want to accomplish the next day that are in line with my business's needs, personal goals, or weekly timeline. I keep it short, and I don't write down tasks that are overly time consuming or unachievable in a day. I used to try to remember what I needed to do in my head, but things just kept building up, making me feel overwhelmed. Obviously, each day is full of many tasks, but identifying the most important ones is a must for your peace of mind. Even if you already have a to-do list from a boss, I suggest you write down your own "sticky note success list" for yourself. This method declutters your mind and keeps daily pressure in check.

Here are some examples of appropriate daily goals:

1) 45-minute workout
   —give it my all
2) Get groceries—stick to budget
and choose healthy options!
3) Grab coffee with "so-and-so"
   —be authentic and engaged.
4) Finish writing the "pressure"
chapter for FindingBetter
5) Read instead of Netflix tonight
   —even if it's only 10mins

Notice that these goals are not *unattainable, exhaustive* goals like working out for two-and-a-half hours or finishing an entire project. Still, be forgiving of yourself on the occasional days that get away from you; this happens to everyone. Also, notice that not every goal is based on productivity. Your list shouldn't only derive from "work, work, and more work." It's a valid goal to write down being a good listener and communicator. There's something empowering by defining the demeanor we hope to have before we interact with people. When we set social goals, we have better interactions throughout the day.

The other important practice is placing an emphasis on going out of your way to impact others. It's easy to get stuck in the "I" mentality as we go through life. *What can "I" do to have a better day? What can "I" do to be more successful?* When we slip into this narrow, self-focused mindset, it becomes all about our journey, and how we can advance our position in life. I feel like I'm preaching to myself here because I easily get stuck in this trap, *fixated on my own journey* and *ignoring the importance of promoting others.*

I recently heard a speaker point out the trend in our culture to focus on "me first" instead of lifting others up. When did we stop fighting for other people—fighting to help them through their day and make an impact on their journey? Impact doesn't start after we have thousands of followers; impact starts by trying to make a difference in one person's life day after day. This is living for the "one" and not the "one thousand." It starts with something as simple as giving an honest compliment, smiling at someone, thanking them for a job well done, or suggesting that "they" deserve a promotion. Actions like these go a long way in the world today. If we can start living like this, then the inward pressure gets displaced and redistributed for the overall good of ourselves and others. I want to live more like this: less focused on myself and more focused on the person who's doing life right next to me.

I want to… **Love. People. Well.**

The world desperately needs this mindset shift. Even if we're facing Depression or Anxiety, we can still set in motion positive change.

This is the pressure we need: a pressure to make a positive difference using our individual lane, coupled with the decision to wake up and continually *love people well.*[4]

The pressure is on.

Sign me up. I'm all in.

TAKEAWAYS

- "Pressure" is good to a point; we have to properly manage it.
- What's your lane (even if it changes over time)? Pressure needs to be redirected in a meaningful direction.
- Each day, set four to five well-rounded goals that pertain not only to productivity, but also to personal interactions and impacting others. That list becomes your simple guide for daily success.
- *Love. People. Well.*

TO DALLAS AND BACK

FRIENDSHIPS/ RELATIONSHIPS

I don't distinctly remember struggling to make friends in elementary school. I guess that's because as kids there's very little behind a solid friendship.

> "Hey, you! Do ya like Power Rangers?"
> "Yeah!"
> "Me too!"
> "You wanna be friends?!"
> "Yeahhh!"

Just like that, you have a new best friend to play lava monster with. (Remember lava monster? Those were the days!)

But as we get older, *finding*, *fostering*, and *maintaining* quality friendships is quite a challenge.

I guess I should clarify. Finding "friends" isn't that hard. Anyone can go to a bar or party, start up a conversation with a coworker or acquaintance, and develop a surface level friendship. Ironically, it's quite similar to the elementary playground conversation—finding basic similarities in each other and running with it. What I mean by "quality friendships" are friends that truly support you, and vice versa. People you can have a good time with, but also who make your life *better*. They build you up and help you grow in the right direction. They bring new depth to your life. They know your whole story... the struggles and all.

If you find a few people like this, then you've got yourself an inner circle. A group of people to do life with.

Are you ready for two sobering statements I've received from influential mentors in my life?

1. You become the average of the five friends you spend the most time with.

2. Show me your friends, and I'll show you your future.

Based on those two statements, your inner circle had better be comprised of people who excel in life. People who are: *authentic, transparent, compassionate, kind, generous, courageous, driven, spontaneous, intelligent, insightful, self-controlled, patient,* and *respectful.* These are words that should describe the people in your inner circle. When you start to bond with friends like this, your life transcends from average to amazing.

———————

When it comes to the process of finding an inner circle, you'll find that your current situation falls into one of three categories:

CATEGORY 1: THE HEALTHY CIRCLE

You already have a group of friends who are quality people. They've got your back through the ups and the downs.

CATEGORY 2: THE SHALLOW CIRCLE

Your friend-group is in contrast to the direction you want your life to go. In fact, you may be reading this chapter and starting to question the dynamics of your "inner circle."

CATEGORY 3: THE YET-TO-BE-BUILT CIRCLE

You want close friends, and you acknowledge the importance of having genuine friendships; however, finding your own inner circle hasn't quite worked out yet.

THE HEALTHY CIRCLE

If you've labeled your friend group as Category One, then thankfully your friends will be a huge factor in *finding better*. Open up with them—if you haven't already – about any struggles or insecurities you're facing. When you go through rough days, let them encourage you. Allow them to hold you accountable to resisting old habits and negative ways of thinking. They will remind you of how far you've already come, and how far you'll continue to climb. However, if you feel like you can't open up to them because you're worried that it would be awkward, or that they would judge you, then maybe your friends are closer to the dynamics of Category Two.

Conversely, know that when one of them comes to you looking for encouragement and advice, your experiences will provide empathy and compassion. Lastly, when a new person reaches out to you in search of friendship, don't be closed-off. You've likely experienced where they're coming from; and therefore, at least get to know them. There should never be a limit to the number of friends in your inner circle as long as it's comprised of good people. Life is better lived with the mindset of building a "community," rather than forming a "country club."

THE SHALLOW CIRCLE

Does the overall *foundation* of your group of friends align with the words laid out on page 88? If not, your current friends might fall into Category Two.

> ➤ **FOUNDATION** *(Context)* A friendship or relationship's *foundation* is the shared similarities, values, and priorities that create the underlying base of connection. *Synonyms:* base, bedrock, cornerstone

Sometimes, it can be hard to tell if the people in our lives are making us better or worse. Your current friends may not be terrible people; they may be fun, they may totally crack you up, and they may always be up for hanging out. But, the more you think about it, they could be keeping you from *finding better*. What actions, activities, and priorities define your friend-group? Could that foundation be side-tracking your life? If we're the average of our five closest friends, then answering these tough questions is important. Who we invest in truly matters.

For many years of my life, my friend-group embodied the qualities of a "shallow circle." Any guidance I offer comes from my first-hand trial and error (and lots of screwing up). It's important for me to note that my closest friends throughout high school, and the first part of college, have no responsibility for the choices I made. My decisions were, and are, 100% my responsibility, as are yours. The challenge is that the habits of our friends gradually become the ones that shape our own habits and decisions. It's almost impossible to go against the grain.

Here are some friendship examples that may seem okay on the surface, but are far from real inner circle material — well tested, by yours truly.

Example 1: The people that you bond with at a before-the-game tailgate party or over a two-day bender. If your friendship revolves around beer die or bottomless mimosas, then I'd be skeptical of that friendship's depth and ability to positively change your life. I'm not saying that going out drinking with friends is wrong, but does it happen on *occasion*, or is it the *consistent foundation* of the friendship? Big difference.

Example 2: The people you initially connect with, but then, every time you talk, conversation is either dominated by them or saturated in negativity. There's a time for listening and letting a friend vent to you, but not all the time. If negativity is such a consistent facet of a person's demeanor that it begins to rub off on your personality, then limit the amount of interaction you have with them.

Example 3: The people you hang with after smoking a couple of bowls. Of course, it may seem like a deep connection when you start to discuss topics while being high, e.g., debating what's the funniest YouTube video, the movie *Inception*, In-N-

Out's secret menu options, or whether Tupac is dead or alive. But in reality, that connection can be mostly smoke and mirrors (pun intended). If smoking blunts is the common bond, then *finding better* may not be the main byproduct of that friendship.

Example 4: The people you naturally bond with, but you quickly realize that they have some sort of odd speech impediment. They use the F-word like it's a noun, verb, adjective, adverb, and preposition all at the same time. This relates to Example 2, since negativity and swearing go hand-in-hand. Of course, cussing is culturally accepted, e.g., stand–up comedy, movies, and music; however, it can cross the line, becoming a negatively embedded characteristic of a friend's personality. If the common saying "everything in moderation" is true, then that applies to our vernacular as well. It's something to think about when analyzing the personalities of your friends, and the intellect/positivity they bring to your life.

These examples may seem a little harsh, but as we get older, we start to notice the effect that people have on our lives. I can't advocate enough for the importance of *filtering friendships*.

And now we make our way to Category Three...

THE YET-TO-BE-BUILT CIRCLE

I have so much empathy for those of you who are currently walking through life without an inner circle. I wasn't lying about my claim at the beginning of this chapter; making friends can be difficult (and even more so, after college).

Maybe you've moved to a new school, job, or city and can't seem to develop a really close crew. Maybe socializing doesn't come easy for you, and things like social Anxiety impede your ability to naturally connect with people. Maybe you've had to make some tough friendship changes, and now, you're trying to connect with new people. Maybe you've recently been through a breakup, leaving a relational hole in your life. Any of these situations may be leading you to search for a new community, but the process might be harder than you ever imagined.

I spent two years in a similar situation—living without close friendships. For some of you, your time without a close group of friends may even be longer. Looking back, I call that time of my life my "season of obscurity."[1]

> ➢ **OBSCURITY:** the state of being unknown, inconspicuous, or unimportant.[2]

This definition may feel like it describes your life right now. There are seasons of life for all of us where loneliness sweeps in, leaving us feeling obscure. While my season of obscurity allowed for some much-needed self-improvement, I continually desired to find a close-knit group of friends like I saw in other people's lives. I had decided to pivot from my prior friend group and the foundation that it was built on. As a result, I went from having many friends to becoming isolated— pretty much having nobody in a matter of six months.

Three years later, I now have a stronger inner circle than I could have ever imagined—one comprised of friendships that are built on a radically different foundation.

How'd I find my new inner circle?

I stretched myself to embrace being *uncomfortable*. This is not usually the word you'd think of when you picture developing close friends. However, the fact is, you cannot grow unless you're uncomfortable (in friendships and in life). Hear me out...

BUILDING FRIENDSHIPS

I'm envious of people who connect with others effortlessly! For 90% of us, even some extroverts, building friendships from the ground up means confronting an ample amount of awkwardness and social Anxiety.

Here are just a couple of prime examples of social elegance (or the lack thereof):

1) Have you ever gone to give someone a "Bro-Shake" with a casually raised hand, and they decide to go with the "No-Nonsense" traditional handshake? The result: ten loooong seconds of finding a mashed-up middle ground, ultimately ending with a clumsy handshake combination. What a way to start a conversation!

2) Or worse, an acquaintance sees you from across the room and comes over to say hi. Your brain has a mini-spasm, and you space their name. Of course, the best thing to do would be to politely ask them for a refresher on their name, but how often do we choose that solution? No, we ride out the conversation by referring to them as, "dude," "man," or "you," until it's over. We can only hope to find them on Facebook later to solve the mystery.

This is classic dysfunctional conversation at its best!

When I left my prior friend-group and set out to build new friendships, I realized that it was going to take much more social confidence than I had exhibited in the past. It would mean embracing plenty of uncomfortable encounters (like the examples above) and overcoming a hesitancy to put myself out there.

Anyone who meets me now, thinks I'm likely an extrovert. Ironically, I'm undoubtedly an introvert at my core. I recharge by being alone and have to limit concentrated social interactions and activities. I easily open up to people I've known for awhile, but being outwardly social in new settings takes intentional effort on my part.

Knowing this about myself, I knew that I'd have to get past my reservations to develop friends. Therefore, I challenged myself to embody the social qualities of an extrovert. I set out with one goal for myself in any social interaction: I wanted to be outgoing, engaging, and conversational so that people would actually think I was a natural extrovert. Don't mistake this as me telling any fellow introverts to disregard their personality. Introverts encompass wonderful qualities, and we're naturally wired one way or the other. But, if you're an introvert you still have to be capable of being bold. Whether you're an introvert or an extrovert, we all have to become an "engager," to seek the meaningful relationships we desire.

––––––––––––

Sometimes we forget how much effort is required to develop a solid friendship. Even once we get past small talk and initial moments of uncomfortableness, it takes continued effort on our part. Building a friendship takes three things: (1) **Initiation** (2) **Time/Energy** and (3) **Balance**.

Building friendships requires becoming an "**initiator**." Don't wait for social opportunities, but instead be willing to try something new, and change your social environment. Join a club, explore nature, find a church, sign up for a rec league, or take a community class. Being an "initiator" means not waiting for someone to text you to do something, or getting a Facebook invite to an event, but rather, initiating connection. Be the one to host a *Super Bowl* party, a *This Is Us* viewing get-together, a backyard BBQ, or a Codenames game night.

Once new friendships have been established, they require **time and energy** to grow. It takes consistently having game nights, watching movies, and going bowling. It means squeezing into a tightly packed Toyota RAV4 and driving 20+ hours to see the one and only Ben Rector perform. (All the way "to Dallas and back" in one weekend. I'll never forget that one!) It means planning ski trips, having lake days, volunteering together, camping in national parks, playing in soccer tournaments, and participating in "all you can eat" wing nights. Each social activity reveals a new depth of authenticity for both you and your friends. This is how a community is created.

Developing this community demands having **balance**. It's choosing to balance your Saturday with personal rest and social plans. It's easy to get accustomed to watching Hulu, or gaming for the majority of the weekend, but *initiators* instigate and prioritize time for interpersonal interaction. They rest when needed, to recharge for the moments that matter. They do their best to balance their social, personal, and vocational lives each week to find harmony.

This entire process doesn't magically happen overnight. Along the way, there will be moments that invariably test every green friendship. But, budding friendships will eventually shift into autopilot.

Not everyone you meet will become a close friend, and that's okay! Give your efforts enough time to identify if their personality and lifestyle fit with yours. If it doesn't work out, no worries. Just keep trying.

RELATIONSHIPS

Taking a slight pivot from friendships, let's tackle topics surrounding relationships. All of what encompasses the word "relationship" (being single, dating, break-ups, falling in love, etc.) affects and is a piece of your inner circle too. If you're dating someone, they will likely be your closest companion in a layered inner circle.

Just like it can take time to find close, lasting friendships, the same can be said about finding someone special. Being single can feel uncomfortable and lonely, but waiting to find the right relationship and working on yourself until then is important.

Whether or not it feels like it, being single can actually be a good thing. You simply CANNOT grow to the extent that you may NEED to if you're in a relationship. I'm not saying that if you're already in a relationship, that's necessarily a bad thing. But, are they "your person" or are they just a relational filler? If you can't see yourself with them long-term, then you might want to reconsider putting energy into that relationship.

Being single is an opportunity to work on yourself relentlessly. As you wait for a true gem to show up in your life, focus your energy on *running your race*.[3] Don't anxiously wonder, *Will I ever find someone?* You will... when the time is right. However, you'd want the future person you're looking for to be continually improving him or herself until they've met you. So, hold yourself to that same standard. *Don't contradict your expectations in your ideal partner* by putting individual growth on hold just because waiting is hard. You have to work on yourself *in the waiting.*

Being single is a gift. It allows you to focus on finding and fostering your inner circle friendships, which takes time to develop. Use your time being single as leverage to maximize these efforts. Use it as motivation to improve areas of your life that may have become stagnant. Find your own identity first instead of looking to find it in a relationship.

––––––––––––

Waiting for a person that's truly a good fit is not easy. Many of us can hurriedly or accidentally settle for someone who might not be the best addition to our lives. This would be someone who comes with red flags, such as their family is toxic, they drink too much, they lack career goals, they neglect their health, they're lazy, they're manipulative, they demand too much from you, or they don't reciprocate equal appreciation and affection. These concerns go unnoticed when we feel lonely. They get buried under *attraction, attention,* and *the desire* to be close to someone. Realize the vulnerability that comes with loneliness, and don't settle for someone who doesn't elevate your life and bring out the best in you. Don't settle for someone that you don't truly connect with. This takes some serious self-control and patience, but the outcome is the priceless assurance that your relationship will not be frivolous.

> **FRIVOLOUS:** not having any serious purpose or value.[4]

Since I'm telling it like it is, I'll take it a bit further. When a couple decides to have sex is their decision. Obviously, there are clear boundaries dependent on age. But assuming that age is not an issue, I encourage you to view sex as a *serious, intimate decision* rather than an *immediate, physical addition*. We're presented the idea through media and culture that sex is a decision that's casual and expected from the beginning. It's portrayed as an emotionally harmless component of any modern relationship. But, it affects us more than we think.

One night stands take sex and cheapen it. As New York Times columnist David Brooks implies so eloquently, viewing sex as something more than casual is to "preserve the loftiness and true beauty of sex, to keep it from being dragged into the materialistic shallowness of the world."[5]

In our world of instant digital connections, it's easy to find someone you're physically attracted to and quickly become sexual with them. But, if you have sex on the first date, second date, or even within the first few months, then likely, the relationship is primarily based on physical attraction, and sex is the foundation. Once we jump to sex, that's the main driving force. It just is. Not to mention, either person can effortlessly go and find more dating options and social profiles that "seem" more appealing.

Purposefully delaying sex can be hard to embrace. There are arguments for both sides. In my opinion and experience, one of the challenges with sex is that it enhances your emotional connection as a couple. This may not seem harmful, but if you're with someone who's not the best fit for you, and sex enters the picture, then it can cloud the perception of the relationship making it seem better than it is. Having sex can compensate for a lack of personality, character, or true compatibility, creating an exaggerated bond with someone. Because of this, red flags can be overlooked.

Putting this perspective into practice requires self-control, but in every aspect of life, when is more self-control not a bad thing? Like, seriously? If a long-term, meaningful relationship is a marathon, then casual sex is a sprint. Both are ways to run, but if you want to train for a marathon—if that's your goal—sprinting won't do anything for you. A long-term relationship may be the last thing on your mind, but I still believe having casual hookups can open the door for additional emotional baggage when you do feel ready to find "your person."

In my opinion, what needs to happen to create a lasting relationship is to develop a genuine friendship first. It's the difference between the relationship being glued together by an Elmer's Glue Stick or by Loctite. That's why the longer you can wait, the better chance you have at a long-term, meaningful relationship.

Truly get to know a person before sex enters the picture. Do life with them. Date them long enough to go through a few seasons (literal seasons like summer, fall, or winter, but also seasons of life—the ups and the downs). Do they treat people well? Are they good with kids? Are they smart with their finances? What are their stances on social issues? How do they act after a fight? (Do they hold a grudge, or are they quick to forgive?)

In fact, fall in love with them before sex. It's absolutely possible to do so. You can know someone is "your person," without sex as evidence for the truth of that love. Ann Landers once said, "Love is a friendship that has caught fire."

Admittedly, I haven't always valued intimacy and love in such a way, but as you grow up, one's perspective on love changes—at least it did for me. I now recognize love as something really special and important.

Falling in love is not to be quickened; it's a journey. First, you really get to know a person, and then you fall in love with who they are. You begin to not only notice the small, quirky traits about them, but you begin to cherish those qualities. Their character becomes evident, and the way they live life is revealed. Conversation is effortless because they're your best friend; they're someone you could spend hours with and not have a single dull moment. Falling in love like this respects the power behind intimacy. It's watching small embers catch fire to become strong, blazing flames. Being a part of that combustion is why falling in love is like nothing else.

In my life, I want to end up with someone who really knows me and vice versa. I want a best friend, a confidant, an adventure partner, an imperfect counterpart, a loyal companion, and a supporter in life's most difficult moments. I hope to find this kind of love and reciprocate it. I'm sure you do too. I think most people do! However, finding this type of exceptional love often requires not settling, and going against the cultural norm.

All of this is not to say that sex is insignificant or avoidable in a relationship. Being attracted to each other is really important. In fact, I'm arguing the opposite. *Intimacy is everything*, which is why it should be treated like it's everything. I'm not saying that holding back a bit on the decision to have sex is easy. When you're in love... you're in loooovvve; feelings run deep. But, love is rarely strengthened when intimacy is cheapened.

———————

Many mistakes marked my first serious relationship. Some were mutual, and some were exclusive to me. I can't say that the old version of myself didn't present some red flags as well. But, we were young and in love—a potential combination for a shaky foundation. Our breakup was one of the hardest things I've ever been through. I wasn't ready to give up; she was. However, looking back, I can't be hard on either of us. I've since found meaning behind that season of my life. So, for those of you who are going through a breakup, know that pain comes first, then improvement, then understanding, peace, and eventually, the opportunity for a fresh start. So keep all of this in mind as you feel tempted to settle, to swipe right, to send an angry message in retaliation, or to flat out give up. This too shall pass, but not before some incredible transformation takes place.

———————

Regardless of where you are with your current inner circle, there's a fundamental truth: The people in our life determine the direction we're headed. Your friendships matter, and so do your relationships. As we continue to chip away at Depression and Anxiety, the ability to know that the people in our lives will support us going forward is paramount.

If I could encourage you in any way during this process of finding and building important connections, it's this:

Be patient.

Stay the course.

It's *in the waiting* that we become who we're truly supposed to be.

TAKEAWAYS

- Sometimes the people around us limit our ability to progress, and conversely, some bring out the best in us. What standards have you set for your friendships, and do they need to be modified?
- To make friends, you have to become an *initiator* who embraces the challenges of communication. Totally worth it.
- Singleness is a gift—a time for major personal growth and grounding. When the right person shows up, you'll be a better version of yourself who has the right tools to build a foundation that will last.

I'D RATHER NOT

· COUNSELING ·

When I scheduled my first professional counseling session, every stereotypical image related to therapy entered my head. I imagined laying back on a brown leather couch, staring up at a blank ceiling, feeling obligated to ramble off my problems. All of this while a therapist wearing Warby Parker frames and a plaid button-up, meticulously jotted down notes about my life... inserting "Freudian-themed" remarks when he or she deemed them appropriate. I mean, this is what we see in most movies, so that's what I was conditioned to expect.

Ironically, what I encountered on my first swing at counseling wasn't far from the stereotype. The only difference was that instead of a notepad, this counselor resorted to a large whiteboard to write down my long list of issues...

Our session began with him pulling out his set of dry erase markers, eager to take notes...

ME: "Wait, what?" I questioned. "You want me to make a pros-and-cons list?

COUNSELOR: "Yes! I think it could be really beneficial for your situation."

ME: "You think a pros-and-cons list would be beneficial to my situation???"

COUNSELOR: "Yes, it's an activity I use with most of my clients, and it really helps. Just give it a shot!"

I said to myself, *I'm here for the next 40 minutes so I might as well give this guy what he wants.*
I began sarcastically thinking to myself...

PROS | CONS

PROS	CONS
PRO—THERE'S NOWHERE TO GO FROM HERE BUT UP.	CON—I'VE NEVER BEEN THIS LOW BEFORE.
PRO—I LEFT COLLEGE EARLY. I NEVER REALLY LIKED IT ANYWAY!	CON—NOW WHAT?!
PRO—MY COUNSELOR'S GREAT AT MAKING PROS-AND-CONS LISTS.	CON—I DON'T REALLY CARE FOR PROS-AND-CONS LISTS.
PRO—I'M ALIVE...	CON—I'M NOT SURE I WANT TO BE!

This is basically what went down for the remainder of my first-ever counseling session. Needless to say, we didn't get very far, and there wasn't some magical breakthrough. Honestly, I was defiantly against opening up to some random person about my life. On top of that, I wasn't even sure how to accurately verbalize my feelings. I just knew I was struggling and couldn't go on living that way anymore. Even so, my parents insisted that I give counseling another try. They hoped I could find a counselor who could truly help guide me as an impartial third party. As you might have guessed, I decided not to stick with the first guy, but I finally agreed to try someone else who was recommended to me.

I started seeing a counselor named Kelley on a bi-weekly basis. The first few sessions were rough. I fought being there and thought that our discussions couldn't benefit me in any way. In fact, before our first session, I was so anxious and resistant that I contemplated leaving the waiting room and bailing on her!

But, I came to realize there was something different about Kelley. Not only was she a good listener, but she was also approachable. Our first session was conducted in an entirely opposite manner from my other counseling experience. She merely had me update her on the last six months of my life: the insecurities I felt, the negative thoughts, the panic attacks, the breakup, the partying... everything. She calmly inserted perfectly timed questions to help engage and encourage me to open up more about how I was feeling. Together, we were able to label what I was struggling with: a serious bout of Depression coupled with unrelenting episodes of Anxiety. Something about her seemed so down-to-earth and genuine that I quickly began to feel more comfortable during our sessions. Over the next few months, we set goals, we discussed alternatives, and we got to the root of my problems.

Kelley is understanding and kind, but she's also not afraid to tell it like it is. She's relatable and modern — current with the challenges our generation faces. She's been through seasons of Depression and Anxiety herself, which is where she draws much of her valuable advice. For all those reasons, she was instrumental in helping me to correctly analyze my thoughts and feelings. She was able to take what I was struggling with the most, talk about it, and leave me with new ideas on how to work through my feelings in the upcoming weeks.

Understandably, counseling is one of the many options that people choose to avoid. I'm not saying that willingly opening up to someone about your struggles is easy; however, I do believe it can be highly beneficial.

Counselors are trained to guide people through tough times, whether it's Depression, Anxiety, eating disorders, relationships, bullying, loss, abuse/trauma, or addiction. What makes it such a valuable tool is the capacity to communicate with an *unbiased, third-party* person who can guide you through a healing process.

If finances are holding you back, then make sure to expand your search. Counseling isn't limited to paid options only. School counselors, a local church pastor, online counseling via video streaming, and national support hotlines are all counseling-based options as well. If you've tried counseling and didn't think it helped, maybe you just haven't found the right person yet. You may have to try out different people until you find the one that feels the most natural. So, like the other "moves" suggested in this book, I urge you to pursue the right counselor as a vital part of working through challenges, healing, and ultimately, *finding better*.

———————

Early in my season of critical Depression and Anxiety, my mom shared with me something that Kelley had told her over a phone conversation.

She said: "Ben will be a better man when he gets through all this... and he will get through this. He'll have a depth of compassion and character that he wouldn't have developed otherwise. He'll see people through a new lens that only comes through experiencing suffering and personal struggle."

PRO — KELLEY WAS RIGHT.

CON — IT SURE AS HELL TOOK A LOT OF WORK!

Thank you, Kelley G., for the time you invested in my life. The world needs more people like you! And for any counselor reading this, thank you for all that you do. Keep showing up!

TAKEAWAYS

- Counseling doesn't have to be an expensive endeavor. Explore all of the possibilities.

- You may have to try a few counselors before you connect with the one that will truly impact your life.

- Opening up to a person about our struggles is tough, but concealing them is worse.

PART III

THE BODY

SHE SAID, "HI!" NOW WHAT?

· FITNESS ·

Do you ever feel like you run into people you know when you're looking your worst?

On a random morning, I'd realize that I was completely out of breakfast food. I figured I could quickly run to the store to get some eggs even though I looked like a total mess. I'd be outfitted in a baggy sweater (circa 1990s), patterned socks, Dad slides, and the world's worst case of bedhead, but what would be the actual chances of running into someone I might know? I mean, come on... it would only take five minutes. Of course, right as I'd walk into the store, BAM... I'd run into an old friend or WHAM... I'd see my former boss. Or even worse, BOOM... I'd stumble into the cute girl from my Psych 101 class. Call it bad luck or bad timing, but it seemed to happen EVERY. DANG. TIME! Thus began my self-established rule: Always be somewhat presentable before going out.

When I came back from my first year of college to start my healing process, I was an absolute wreck and, in my mind, *far from presentable*. I felt like I was in no condition to see anyone I knew, nor did I want to. I couldn't bear the thought of having a BAM, WHAM, or BOOM moment. For one thing, I was so embarrassed about my severe acne that I could barely hold a conversation. My social Anxiety was off the charts because I felt like I wasn't good enough to be seen by anyone. As much as I wanted to look "cut" like Michael B. Jordan, my physique was quite the opposite. Two semesters of heavy partying and dorm food wasn't "cutting" it.

But on a deeper level, I didn't want to have to explain to anyone I knew why I was back from college early, or why I was living with my parents again. I didn't want to have to fake an answer for someone questioning, "What's your plan now? What do you want to do with your life?" I didn't want to have to field questions of curiosity from high school friends about my breakup. And externally, I truly did look and feel *exhausted*, *depleted*, and quite frankly... *different*. I was struggling and didn't want people to know. My self-confidence was completely shot.

After sitting down with my family and having a heart-to-heart about how I was feeling, we created a list of things to do to help me build my self-esteem back up. You can imagine how reluctant I was at first about my family's suggestion to get a membership at the local gym. I was barely doing well enough to consider setting health-related goals. However, the number one thing on the list was to start working out. I knew the traditional benefits included getting stronger and losing a few pounds, but beyond that, I felt like working out was something I needed to do. I felt that if I could get in shape, my confidence would be boosted, and I might be able to make it through the valley I was walking in. I wanted to look better and needed goals to strive toward to divert my mind from Depression and Anxiety.

> Sidenote: That's probably the worst thing about getting in shape: the few months of looking at yourself in the huge wall-sized mirrors, reminding you of how far you still need to go to reach your goals! Is it not?

When I began looking at gyms to join, I decided to pick a small one that was farther away from my house than the two closest mega-fitness centers. This was a strategic decision to avoid running into anyone I knew. The gym was open 24/7, which was another benefit. I found myself developing a rhythm of working out late at night. This helped my

Anxiety and allowed me to "get in the zone" without being crowded by lots of people. These late-night sessions became my quiet time, mirroring something that could be considered meditative and resetting. I felt that if I could work out peacefully, I'd have a better shot at accomplishing my goals— and I was right. Much of the hard work required to change who I was on the inside, and the outside, happened at this little gym. Lodged between an old Chinese restaurant and a tattoo shop, it could easily go unnoticed. This place may not have been the most glamorous, boutique-type fitness studio, but nonetheless a priceless part of my journey.

After a couple of months, I began to love going to work out. It was something that I felt good about completing. Most weeks, I worked out at least four days, sometimes even five. But before my physique even started to change, just the accomplishment of breaking a sweat was enough to lift my spirit. Sure, other people were working out as well; it was never an empty gym. But, no one knew me. They didn't know that they were lifting dumbbells next to a kid who couldn't finish his second semester of college. They didn't care about my acne because they hadn't previously seen me without it. And as for Depression and Anxiety, as many can relate, that's something I kept hidden on the inside for no one to see. There was no pressure for me to be perfect or to try and hide my insecurities. I just went to the gym, did my thing, and left feeling better than before. Fast-forward and that newfound passion led me to become a personal trainer in the world of health and wellness.

I cannot emphasize enough how impactful fitness can be on your journey to overcome Depression or Anxiety. At the time, I didn't understand the scientific reasons of why working out helped me to feel so much better. Now I know!

Exercise affects the brain on a biochemical level; it's literally like a free dose of antidepressant medication. Duke University compared the effects of a popular SSRI antidepressant medication to that of moderately working out. They found that "exercise was just as good as medicine."[1] In their study, "Those who exercised at a moderate level — about 40 minutes three-to-five days each week — experienced the greatest antidepressant effect."[2]

But why is this?

"Exercise not only increases blood flow to the brain, [but] it releases endorphins, the body's very own natural antidepressant. It also releases other neurotransmitters, like serotonin, which lift mood."[3]

Another interesting byproduct of activity is that the "brain-derived neurotrophic factor, a chemical that promotes brain health and memory, is also reduced in Depression, and exercise has been found to elevate levels of this neurotransmitter."[4]

Don't confine "working out" to just going to a gym. Health.com defines the powerful link behind physical and mental health as, "The body is the mind and the mind is the body."[5] The editorial staff found that running, hiking, and yoga were three just as powerful exercise solutions to fight Depression and Anxiety. For example, running "causes lasting changes in our 'feel good' neurotransmitters serotonin and norepinephrine, both during and after exercise."[6] And the "repetitive motions of running appear to have a meditative effect on the brain."[7] In a study published by the Environmental Health and Preventive Medicine journal, it was found that hiking and immersing oneself in nature vs. walking in the city leads to "lower stress hormone levels."[8]

As for yoga, "besides the stretching and core strengthening, there is a tremendous focus on breathing, which helps to slow down and calm the mind."[9] Experts believe that "yoga's focus on the breath is especially beneficial for your mental health because it's difficult to be anxious when you're breathing deeply."[10]

Recognizing the benefits presented by these findings, I always make sure to encourage my personal training clients to add alternative physical activities outside our scheduled weekly sessions. Whether it be swimming, snowshoeing, rock climbing, kickboxing, cycling, or playing pickup basketball, you have to find ways to get your body consistently moving to reap the incredible antidepressant effects exercise has on the brain.

One of the hardest workouts I've ever done was opposite of the traditional weight lifting and cardio that some people assume is the best option. I eagerly signed up for a Hot Yoga class along with a friend who was already a big fan of the workout. I took the class expecting it to be an hour of relaxed stretching with the bonus of an atmospheric sauna. Boy, was I wrong! That class kicked my butt! Within the first ten minutes, I was confident that my body was not designed to move and stretch like that. The rest of the class participants were smoothly transitioning from pose-to-pose, while I was in the back, sweating bullets, and holding on to the wall to keep myself from cramping up and falling over! I left that class with a whole new level of appreciation for yoga. On top of that, I noticed that every person in that class was fit, lively, and focused. Yoga was their passion, and probably for some of them, maybe even their medication.

––––––––––––––

For one reason or another, people tend to have high initial resistance to exercise. When it comes to your motivational drive to work out, it might seem insanely challenging to get yourself to the gym. Many people succumb to inconsistency and never quite make it past the required time for it to become beneficial and likable. Your ability to develop a workout routine comes down to finding an activity that you like. That might seem basic, but from a personal trainer's standpoint, people rarely choose to initiate it. Just because your best friend loves to run, doesn't mean you have to fake a passion for running and sign up for the next 5k. I challenge you to search for an activity that lights you up—one that sets you on fire and motivates you to keep improving yourself.

Look at all the fantastic fitness companies such as Peloton, Core Power Yoga, Orangetheory, SoulCycle, Pure Barre, Rumble Boxing, and nationwide CrossFit clubs. All of which embrace their own unique, innovative approach to help people get in shape. Or, check out the innovative health and wellness apps flooding the digital marketplace, such as Freeletics, Sworkit, Nike Training Club, PEAR, Daily Burn, and Couch to 5K that are designed to offer fitness guidance. Or for that matter, the thousands of YouTube fitness videos that offer routines and advice as well. There's never been a time in history where we've had this kind of explosion of options and expertise to choose from. Find what makes you tick!

If you take the scientific research from this chapter and combine that with a weekly routine tailored to your level and liking, then working out can become a significant force for improvement. It's good for more than just Depression and Anxiety. The added benefit is that after a few months you'll start to *look* and *feel* better, e.g., energy levels, range of motion, and ability to focus. And whether or not we like to admit it, our confidence in our appearance is another integral factor in being able to beat personal insecurities.

———————————

As for my initial attempt to go incognito and avoid any awkward social run-ins during my lowest season, my plan sort of fell apart. After a couple of weeks of working out under the radar, my social skills were eventually tested. A new front desk attendant was hired whose job was to scan everyone into the gym. She was incredibly cute and personable. Plus, she was into fitness, which was quickly becoming a passion of mine too. Needless to say, I was crushin' hard!

Even though I had the lowest self-confidence of my life, I felt that I had to at least attempt a conversation. I immediately started to overanalyze the whole situation. *What if she notices my acne?*

What if she thinks I look young? What if I say something stupid? This was exactly what I was trying to avoid… any human contact!

But there was no way around it!

One day, I walked in determined to say hi instead of quickly scanning my card and rushing past the desk. I envisioned having "Matthew McConaughey-like" swagger, empowering me to *casually* hold a *simple conversation* with this girl. I stepped up and before I could say anything, she energetically said, "Hi! How are you doing today?"

I panicked…

That was not the plan I had envisioned. I was planning on asking her; I was going to go for it first! I wasn't prepared for the reverse to happen. That small interaction threw me off!

Without even thinking, I nervously blurted out some random, jumbled up phrase that went something like this…. "*Uhhh huginn snieffen*" (which is gibberish for "what the heck am I saying?")

She looked at me like I was crazy (which I kind of felt like I was).

Mortified, I bolted to the men's locker room shaking my head, wishing that I could completely disappear.

"Come on Bennnn!" I thought to myself.

So much for my supposed foolproof plan of going to the gym, doing my thing, and leaving unnoticed and unembarrassed.

Looking back, I can't help but laugh at myself. Honestly, for where I was in life, the courage to even conjure up a plan for a conversation was a huge step for me.

After that, I chose to endure the forevermore awkward scan-in process for the remainder of my time at that gym. I knew that I needed to stick to my goal of becoming a healthier version of myself if I was ever going to feel better mentally and emotionally.

Working out helped to slowly mend some of my brokenness and shift my mindset. It helped me to start treating my body in a way that was conducive to internal and external happiness. Now, three years later, my determination to get and stay in shape has been a chief contributor to *finding better*.

Working out is not solely about improving your physique. I firmly believe that exercise is one of the top three most effective "moves" to combat how you're emotionally feeling. During your journey to develop better health, happiness, and social confidence, improving yourself through exercise and movement may be the most important priority. So, make a move to invest in your health. Bet on yourself to make it through this season, even if there are initial setbacks and resistance.

Who knows? Maybe you'll even meet someone special working at the front desk... and actually be able to say, "Hi" back!

TAKEAWAYS

- Following through with fitness goals is paramount; they come with an initial wall of inevitable resistance, but eventually turn into a game-changer against Depression and Anxiety.
- Movement is medicine.

TYPICAL TIMELINE

First week: Hardest thing ever.

First Month: Still really hard!

Six Months: Challenging, but a noticeable change in appearance, mood, and confidence.

One year: A completely new you who looks good, feels great, and actually appreciates being active and healthy.

(You can't Amazon Prime health and wellness.)

A GIFT FROM GRANNY FRANNY

· NUTRITION ·

When I turned fifteen, I was given the option of saving up to purchase a car of my choice or driving a '97 Cutlass Oldsmobile passed down from my quirky Grandmother (or as we called her—Granny Franny). Don't get me wrong, I appreciated the option to have my first car given to me. But, as a high school boy who was highly influenced by the opinions of his peers, a prune colored paint job, faded leather seats, and a distinct mothball interior aroma just wouldn't do. I pictured myself asking out my high school crush to get half-priced Sonic shakes, but I couldn't bear the image of pulling up in that painfully aged car.

Needless to say, I refused the Oldsmobile and opted to spend that entire year dedicated to earning money for a sweet ride. By my sixteenth birthday, I had successfully saved enough cash to scout used car dealerships for something that I would be proud of. After weeks of looking, I found the car! She was beautiful; everything that a sixteen-year-old boy could ask for.

A few days after my birthday, I bought a bold, red Mitsubishi Lancer. Now, it wasn't a high-end edition, it wasn't souped-up, and it wasn't new, but to me, it was perfect. The car was all mine! I left the car lot beaming, smiling from ear to ear. For the rest of high school, I took amazing care of that car. I made sure to consistently clean and polish the exterior, vacuum and condition the interior, and obsessively change the oil. Oh, and let's not forget, hanging some "Black Ice" tree air fresheners from the mirror to make sure my ride smelled exceptional.

In many ways, our body is like a car. It may seem weird to make that comparison, but hear me out. I treated my first car so well. I made sure to always take care of it so that it would run properly. What we forget to acknowledge about our bodies is that, similar to a car, how we take care of it, and what we put into it, determines how we feel and function. We all know that if you neglect putting oil in a car and continue to run the engine, it will break down. If we drive a car without the correct type of fuel, it will break down. And, if we overlook that weird crunching sound coming from the transmission, you guessed it... the car will break down.

Likewise, your body depends on you taking daily action to keep it running properly. *Everything* that you put into your body causes a reaction for better or for worse. A Harvard Medical School publication confirmed that "there is a link between what one eats and our risk of Depression [and Anxiety]. What we eat matters for every aspect of our health, but especially our mental health."[1] With this reality, the best one-liner to live by is this:

Your *inputs* determine your *output*.

If we find ourselves struggling with Depression and Anxiety, many times we overlook the daily inputs that could be causing that stress (output) on our mind and body.

For example, if your input is the combination of regularly eating fast food, processed snacks, soda, and sugary desserts, then your body's output will resemble the quality of those nutritional choices. Instead, let's say you choose to eat colorful vegetables, fresh food, organic options, and fewer desserts. You drink coffee instead of energy drinks, and you drink an ample amount of water throughout the day. Instead of three or four alcoholic drinks, maybe you only have a couple or skip it altogether. Now, your output will become completely different; the health of your mind and body radically change for the better.

Many people want to beat their Depression and Anxiety, and yet, they continue to neglect to change their nutritional inputs. As a result, they see little progress. As a person who used to devour Taco Bell, stuffing down Beefy 5-layer Burritos with ease (paired with a Baja Blast Freeze as an obvious combo), I finally realized that my dietary choices were affecting my body's emotional and physical output. My habit of drinking Red Bulls and Rockstars in an attempt to get myself going was, in all actuality, the very thing increasing the inefficiency of my body.

Consuming subpar foods and drinks is like charging our phones to 60%, and then pulling the plug. With this approach, we go through each day running down our battery to empty. Conversely, consuming the right foods and drinks will fully recharge us. The result is a sustained battery starting at 100% that no longer consistently dips into the red.

Your age doesn't matter; the choice to live and eat healthily should start as early as possible. It becomes the foundation from which you can better fight Depression and Anxiety.

———————

Backing up the "your *inputs* determine your *output*" equation, the California Institute of Technology and the Clinical Psychopharmacology and Neuroscience research group found that "90% of serotonin is made in our digestive tract."[2] Serotonin is a neurotransmitter that contributes to our feelings of well-being and happiness. It's critical to the health of our brain and the regulation of our sleep and mood. It was once thought that serotonin was only made in the brain, but new research has proved otherwise. If we make poor dietary choices, we compromise the condition and efficiency of our digestive tract, thus impacting the production of much-needed serotonin. A problematic dysfunction of brain-chemical production starts in the gut, not in the mind like previously thought.

Add to that the research-based conclusions from scholars like Dr. Rhonda Patrick (Founder of FoundMyFitness) and Dr. Ed Bullmore (Head of the Department of Psychiatry at the University of Cambridge) that show "in relation to mood, beyond reasonable doubt, there is a very robust association between inflammation and depressive symptoms. Inflammation can cause Depression."[3] When our inner body experiences systemic inflammation, symptoms of Depression and Anxiety arise. But what causes this inflammation, and how can we fix it? Well, the two drivers of internal inflammation are a *poor diet* and *stress*. Any level of internal inflammation disrupts the body's ability to make necessary chemicals that regulate our mind and body.

Dr. Bullmore states that lifestyle changes like "eliminate[ing] processed foods"[4] can help fight Depression and Anxiety, "especially sugar and refined carbohydrates which may increase inflammation in the body."[5] Instead, we should "eat plenty of natural foods including fruits and vegetables."[6]

This new scientific research is essential for a deeper understanding of nutrition versus Depression and Anxiety, but for you and me, let's just stick to the simple one-liner as the guide to our nutritional approach:

Your *inputs* determine your *output*.

If your inputs are less than exceptional, then I challenge you to take action against depleted energy levels or feelings of stress. While it's not easy to change at first, your dietary choices will become a powerful "move" against Depression and/or Anxiety.

WAYS TO MAKE THIS HAPPEN:

- Define what your relationship with food looks like. Do you have a hard time controlling your cravings? Do you eat fast food multiple times a week? Do you feel like you can't go without dessert? Depending on your answers to these questions, set new boundaries for yourself, change the way you shop, or seek nutritional counseling to work through an unhealthy relationship with food.

- Find nutritional websites that regularly post healthy recipes so you know what to eat, and how to make it. Some examples of sites with great content include: skinnytaste.com, eatthis.com, and foodnetwork.com/healthy.

- Download a nutritional app to track your daily choices and consumption. Acknowledging what you eat helps you make better, more proactive choices each week. Great apps include: MyFitnessPal, MyPlate, or SparkPeople Calorie Tracker

- Give yourself a weekly challenge. Try picking something each week that you cut out. *This week I'm cutting out soda. This week I'm not going to have any chips.* You'll realize that it's not as hard as it seems to modify our diets a little bit at a time.

Treat your body like a brand new, sleek Mercedes Benz or a state-of-the-art Tesla. It's something that you should take pride in, and work to improve daily. I mean, if you think about it, we only get one body, and one life... so choose to live healthily. I wish I had never neglected my nutritional habits, but it's now one of my highest priorities.

As for Kate (yes, I named her), I drove the Lancer for two-and-a-half years during high school; two amazing years of luxuriously taking care of that car. Unfortunately, toward the end of my first year of college, I crashed her. I was so clouded by Depression and Anxiety that on my way to the local Taco Bell, I mindlessly ran a red light and T-boned another vehicle. Luckily, everyone involved in the crash was okay. However, Kate was beaten up and needed some major repairs.

When I came home, the only working car available to drive was that damn 1997 Cutlass Oldsmobile! So much for looking cool in a red sports car...

Ironically, I was destined all along to drive that ancient Oldsmobile off into the horizon. Thank you, Granny Franny. :)

TAKEAWAYS

- Your *inputs* determine your *output.*
- We all know what healthy eating looks like, but it's a daily choice to eat healthy foods. What shouldn't be a choice is letting Depression and Anxiety be magnified because of something that we can control (like nutrition).
- The majority of our "mood-determining" brain chemicals are made in the digestive tract (not the brain!), so how we treat nutrition directly affects the body's ability to produce those much-needed chemicals.
- You only have one body and one life; treat it well! Treat it like you would a luxury car.

SAY YES...

ALCOHOL/
MARIJUANA

Mine was peach-flavored Triple Sec. What was yours? You know—the first drink you ever had? I don't mean a sip of your dad's beer or communion wine. I mean, what was the first drink you ever *really* had? Maybe, it was paying someone older than you to buy a six-pack of Lime-A-Ritas from the corner liquor store. Or maybe, you and some friends pooled together what you knew would go unnoticed from the liquor cabinet, making a gross assortment of Jamison, red wine, and Tito's vodka to try. (a.k.a. my sister!) Beggars can't be choosers! For me, it was getting drunk at a sleepover in the 10th grade. A group of us were feeling extra courageous and decided to steal a bottle of alcohol from the parents' cupboard. The first thing we got our hands on was a bottle of peach-flavored Triple Sec. We started to pass the bottle around, each of us taking small sips of the sweet liquor. My first couple of hesitant sips turned into big gulps. I was determined that night to know what alcohol felt like — what being "drunk" felt like. That did the trick! I didn't even make it to 9 p.m. before I was throwing up on my friend's couch. I eventually rallied to join in rambling off Hoodie Allen song lyrics with my collective group of buzzed friends. I'll never forget that night.

I wanted to know what was so forbidden about this liquid that only adults could legally enjoy. Maybe that's why we all remember our first drink because it signified a rite of passage. It made us feel mature. It made us feel invincible. Drinking under 21 is thrilling, risky even... and honestly, fun! But for a majority of our generation, this infatuation with drinking doesn't end once our ID's become horizontal. At least for me, that first memorable night of true drinking marked the beginning of a relationship that wasn't healthy or balanced. It certainly didn't push me to *find better*. For a long time, I didn't want to admit that. At first, it was because I honestly didn't believe it, and then later, because I didn't want to deal with the implications of it being true.

Fast-forward a year, and by the time I was a junior in high school, gone were the days of trying things for the first time. I was accustomed to drinking alcohol as well as smoking marijuana. It was a huge part of who I was, and it was a crucial component in my definition of a "good time." When I graduated high school, partying was one of my main priorities for the college experience I desired. I chose to leave home in search of full independence and looked forward to the freedom to party on my terms. No more sneaking in late at night, or trying to convince Mom and Dad that I was sober. I ended up at your typical state school with Division 1 sports, an extensive campus, and ***ding ding ding*** plenty of parties. I quickly ramped up my drinking habits to an average of four days a week, and I immersed myself in the common "party culture" found across our nation.

As young adults, this "party culture" we face is a very real thing. Collectively, our generation's relationship with partying seems to be more elevated than previous ones. It's exceedingly prevalent and steadily pursued. In my opinion, the key thing to note is the difference between two words: *activity* versus *culture.*

An *activity* is something you partake in every once in a while, and then leave it to return to a routine. It's not something that defines you or something that becomes a huge priority or habit.

Culture is the embedded lifestyle of a group of people. Something that's cultural occurs frequently.

It's a *part* of the routine. It's a consistent priority of the group.

Drinking and smoking, and more, have begun to shift from being merely an *activity* to becoming a *cultural part* of our generation's identity. This shift can be seen on social media, found on most college campuses, and many high schools as well. It's not only occurring on the weekends, but daily in cities and rural areas alike. After college, this cultural lifestyle continues. You may find yourself working at a millennial-based company where coworkers set aside Thursday, Friday, and Saturday nights for hitting up the bars after work. Happy hour is part of the routine, except now, Keystones are replaced with craft beer.

My relationship with partying expressed this major difference between "culture" and "activity." As a college freshman, I honestly believed that I could party every week, have loads of fun, and not be functionally affected in any way (outside of the occasional hangover). I bought into the belief that consistent partying can be a sustainable routine. This same false expectation confronts many young adults. As long as we can handle class, work, and partying, then we're all good. But, it's never that simple.

This culture of partying has been enhanced by a "party lifestyle" presented through social media, music, and other forms of media. Party-driven content makes this lifestyle seem manageable and desirable—maybe even the best way to live life as a young adult.

Having fun has become directly associated with drinking and smoking. I fell victim to this narrow-view. I admittedly thought any social outing or event needed to be paired with a few drinks to enrich the experience. For a long period of my life, the friend group I felt closest to lived similarly. Whether it was a movie, bowling, or playing volleyball in the park, every fun activity was partnered with drinking or smoking.

In my story, my habits surrounding alcohol and marijuana did catch up with me. Both substances became clear factors in the increasing "perfect storm" I found myself in. Drinking and smoking allowed Depression and Anxiety to creep into my life, further clouding my emotional outlook. I had to become the detective of my own feelings to see this. The evidence was buried below the surface of late nights and crowded house parties in a "pursuit of happiness." Eventually, I found that my Depression and Anxiety were not only linked to, but also magnified by, alcohol and marijuana. It took some hardcore self-analysis to see that both were destroying my ability to find stability... and steady happiness.

Alcohol and marijuana kept me from correctly dealing with how I was feeling. That's the most important thing to realize about these substances: For all the qualities that make them so appealing, they can prevent us from dealing with issues and insecurities in the right way. We need to confront stress, loneliness, social Anxiety, and any other challenging feelings through self-reflection, and then personal and environmental change. Alcohol and marijuana, if mishandled, offer a fractured solution by numbing and deflecting feelings, providing only temporary relief in life's tough situations. This never leads to *finding better*. Paraphrasing the wise words that civil rights leader, F.L. Hamer, said, "sometimes you have to be sick and tired of being sick and tired to make a change."

The most important thing is that you become the detective of your own story. Is alcohol or marijuana contributing to your "storm?" For me, close to 50% of my storm was being affected by my partying habits. It's different for each of us, and it's something only you can determine.

The rest of this chapter describes how alcohol and marijuana affect our emotional state on a physiological level. We're all adults here. We can set our own boundaries. This information just enables you to better evaluate your own life and establish a relationship with them based on the research.

———

ALCOHOL AS IT'S RELATED TO ANXIETY AND DEPRESSION:

The reason we feel so good when we drink is because "alcohol mimics the effects of neurotransmitters like GABA that help us feel relaxed and chill."[1] However, have you ever felt more anxious the day after? That's because during the next day, the "effects are reversed, causing anxiety to spike."[2] It's a total shift. In fact, the same spike and drop happens with the serotonin (a happiness hormone) that alcohol releases. When we binge on alcohol, we will inevitably feel more anxious the next day. When I used to drink and overdo it, I dealt with these notable mental shifts. I wasn't aware of this connection. It took a while for me to recognize that the drinking that temporarily "made me feel better" was actually a big reason I ultimately felt worse.

MARIJUANA AS IT'S RELATED TO ANXIETY AND DEPRESSION:

While many people believe that marijuana can alleviate certain symptoms like Anxiety or Depression, new studies evaluating its long-term effect on our emotions contradict that cultural belief. A new 2019 study, conducted with 23,317 adolescents, laid to rest the debate over whether or not marijuana affects our mental state. Researchers found that cannabis use during the teenage years was associated with a nearly "40 percent bump in the risk of depression and a 50 percent increase in the risk of suicidal thoughts in adulthood."[3] Compare this research to the statistic that "1 in 5 young adults smoke marijuana," and you can see that this very well may be a chief contributor to the rapid increase in our culture's Depression and Anxiety.[4]

An interesting reaction called the "rebound effect" is now being associated with consistent marijuana use.[5] Basically, when people feel anxious, they use cannabis to benefit from its calming high. But after continued use, the brain—and body—learns that it typically receives cannabis when it feels symptoms of Anxiety (because our brains are freakin' smart and adapt to everything). Then, the brain starts initiating Anxiety, worry, and feelings of stress when a person isn't high, to trigger them to use cannabis again. Before they know it, they're anxious all the time because their brain and body have learned to intensify their emotions in order to get a substance it craves.

CBD — a nonpsychoactive cannabinoid that is extracted from marijuana/hemp plants — may be an exception to these findings. CBD products offer positive benefits without getting someone high. CBD may help relieve the effects of stress and Anxiety, as well as having anti-inflammatory properties.[6] The general stance on CBD from a scientific standpoint is that more research is needed before clear conclusions can be made.[7] Nonetheless, it's an alternative with intriguing promise.

Because of my conclusion that drinking and smoking were affecting my Depression and Anxiety, I decided to give them up. Originally, I thought I would only pause my relationship with alcohol and marijuana long enough to get back on my feet after coming home from my year out of state. However, after some time had passed, I tried drinking again and the results were the same. Twice I drank too much. On the third time. I didn't overdo it, but I still felt mentally worse the following day. I stopped because of this simple realization: drinking led me to *not think enough*, and smoking weed led me to *think too much*. I needed more consistency with my mind and emotions and both substances kept me from being able to do so.

Not drinking is a part of who I am now—a part of me that I've come to really respect. I haven't had a drink or smoked in three years.

If you had told my younger self that someday I would live sober, and actually enjoy it, I'd bust out laughing.

"No way!" I'd have assuredly responded.

But, here I am.

In a way, I now encounter a different type of self-confidence when offered a drink and politely turn it down. When people (young adults especially) find out that I choose not to drink, it's rarely with judgment, but instead with a reaction of intrigue and admiration. There's a sense of pride found in standing securely in your individual decisions.

This chapter wasn't written to persuade you to give up alcohol or marijuana; that's just what I have chosen to do in my life. That's my story, and it's all I've got, so I'm sticking with it! Your story is different and so are your choices.

My intent was to highlight that both substances do affect us physiologically, especially as frequency and quantity of use increase. Also, I passionately feel that our culture encourages drinking and smoking as a viable part of one's routine. However, to me, *finding better* is sidestepping this cultural vibe and setting up your own lifestyle that is conducive to personal success. *Finding better* in the context of substance use is realizing the difference between consuming from a starting place of contentment versus indulging to curb social Anxiety or to *feel* better.

Developing a healthy relationship with alcohol and marijuana requires establishing intentional lifestyle boundaries that are unique to you.

Sure…
- *Say yes* to having a cold one when catching up with a friend.
- *Say yes* to enjoying a Mojito while relaxing on the beach.
- And with the new legalizations of marijuana, *say yes* in moderation if that's your thing.

But…
- *Say no* if every time you drink you end up overdoing it.
- *Say no* if every social activity involves drinking.
- And, *say no* if you have a relationship with alcohol or marijuana that's disrupting your potential.

The motto for my new life, and quite honestly this chapter, is: choose to fully *find better*, rather than periodically *feeling* better.

Feeling better is temporary.

Finding better is lasting.

TAKEAWAYS

- Both alcohol and marijuana *do* affect us physiologically.
- Partying has become a cultural part of our generation. Sidestep the cultural lifestyle to set-up boundaries with alcohol and marijuana that are conducive to your *own* success and mental health.
- Say "yes" to finding a healthy balance with alcohol and marijuana. Say "no" to letting alcohol and marijuana jeopardize your emotions and personal growth.

MILLIGRAMS & MISCONCEPTIONS

MEDICATION/ SUPPLEMENTS

The following information is not a substitute for medical advice and is not a fully sufficient guide for your decisions as it pertains to prescribed medications and other supplements. I'm not a doctor, and therefore, if you choose to act on any of the advice provided in this chapter, you should first seek official medical approval by your healthcare provider and physician.

ANTIDEPRESSANT MEDICATION

When people use the term "antidepressants," they are typically referring to prescribed medication that treats both Depression and Anxiety. The main antidepressant categories are as follows: SSRI, SNRI, Benzodiazepines (which are focused more on short-term management of Anxiety), and Tricyclic antidepressants.

Each category of medication addresses symptoms through a relatively similar approach by attempting to provide the brain with more serotonin (and other mood-affecting neurotransmitters). This result is accomplished by either increasing neurotransmitter production, or by preventing a breakdown of the pre-existing supply of neurotransmitters, thus leaving more neurotransmitters for the brain to utilize.

When it comes to medication regarding Depression and Anxiety, a wide range of murky information dominates the Internet. Maybe you've heard that taking medication is the absolute best solution for healing, or maybe you've heard that it's the worst. The spectrum of stories, studies, and side effects make for a challenging process when faced with the decision of whether or not to try medication; should I or should I not?

Here's what I've found to be some of the most *common misconceptions* of medication:

MISCONCEPTION #1:

Antidepressants are a cure-all. You can take a pill and everything will quickly get better.

Antidepressants are usually not a quick solution! Some people hurriedly get on an antidepressant, expecting transformation to happen overnight. The misconception is that the antidepressants will rapidly lift one's mood similar to how Advil effectively curbs a minor headache, or how Claritin quickly clears up seasonal allergies. This is not true for antidepressants!

With the exception of Benzodiazepines, these drugs require a long-term process. On average, it takes a full month to even start noticing small changes in mood and demeanor. And then, *it can take a year or more* to fully see the entirety of the medication's benefit on the brain and body.

One of the mistakes I made when taking medication was questioning its effect on me every day. Imagine a kid in the backseat of a family van annoyingly asking, "Are we there yet? Are we there yet? How about now... are we there yet?" I was doing that same thing but instead, questioning, "Is the medication working? Do I feel better yet?" My sister rightfully called me out, stating the truth that, "It's going to take some time! If you wonder whether it's helping you or not every single day, you'll overanalyze to the point of exhaustion." She was right. The change an antidepressant gives you from day-to-day can be minuscule, so be careful not to judge its effectiveness too obsessively.

The notion that antidepressants are a cure-all also creates another problem. This misconception gives people the false belief that they can take a pill, change nothing else in their life, and receive full relief and recovery. When I first took medication, I was thinking that the pill alone would powerfully boost my brain and turn things around. However, even though I was taking it every day, I was living an unhealthy lifestyle. I was drinking, smoking, and partying. I was eating poorly. I was guzzling down energy drinks, soda, and rarely drinking enough water. I was staying up too late, completely draining myself. And, I wouldn't consider changing my social environment, even though my friends' habits were detrimental to my stability. The truth is, a pill can't come close to offsetting bad habits.

MISCONCEPTION #2:

Antidepressants are a crutch and a sign of weakness. It's shameful to be on medication because it means you weren't strong enough to fix your situation on your own.

This was my most misconstrued view of medication. I've always sought to have control over my life and myself. I stubbornly like to do things my way. As I said earlier, it took me seven months just to admit that I was struggling with Depression and Anxiety. In the same way, I fought taking antidepressants with similar resistance. After an adverse reaction while trying an initial antidepressant (which I'll talk about later in this chapter), I went a full year without medication. My strong determination to *find better* on my own led me to attempt healing through other options first.

Within a year, I was able to recover to about 80% by making all of the other "moves" presented in this book. After that year, I felt that I had hit a plateau, so my counselor suggested that I try medication one more time, this time choosing one from a different category. I fought her advice with the belief that medication was a crutch. Just the idea of taking a pill to adjust my mood stirred up shame within me. I felt like I wasn't able to "fix myself" on my own; I felt weak. Her response was this...

> "Your brain is just like any other organ in your body. If your heart needed high-cholesterol medication, you wouldn't hesitate to fill a prescription. However, just because it's your mind, you feel like taking medication is a sign of failure. That's a lie! There's no difference. You need to treat your mind like any other part of your body and consider using the right medication to fully get better."

This feeling—that taking medication is a sign of weakness—is a natural thought for anyone. Many people feel the shame I felt when pursuing medication as a viable option for *finding better*. To put this all in perspective, I fractured my L4 and L5 vertebrae in a sports-related injury during my freshman year of high school. It took 6 months of restricted movement, outside of minimal walking, to recover. Talk about feeling weak! Even having experienced that injury, I felt *even weaker* when I was discussing antidepressant medication options with my doctor. That's how powerful the stigmas are surrounding antidepressants. Don't jeopardize your journey toward better because of a stigma-based misconception.

MISCONCEPTION #3:

Two extremes: *Medication is dangerous and/or highly addictive* or the opposite, *that medication is 100% completely safe.*

My first attempt at trying medication was a quick stint with a SSRI called citalopram (Celexa). I started taking the medication during my final months as a freshman in college, hoping that I'd start to feel better. The opposite happened, and I experienced a negative reaction to the drug. My Depression and Anxiety ramped up. It took about a month to see this effect, but once it started to happen, it was an exponential shift. I was also on Benzodiazepines as a short-term solution for my panic attacks. It's unknown if the two negatively reacted to each other, or if they independently presented side effects. Either way, I decided to get off both after a couple of scary nights where my thoughts elevated from depressed to suicidal. I share this to stress the importance of monitoring your reaction if you choose to try a medication. Everyone has a unique reaction to each category and brand of drug. Always report unforeseen side effects or suicidal thoughts to your doctors immediately. That's why a *well-planned, thought-out* approach, monitored by a physician, is so important if you try medication.

Additionally, let someone close to you know that you're trying a medication before doing so. My parents helped to monitor the process. They actually spotted the mental shift a week before I did. Because changes in Depression and Anxiety can be hard to pinpoint and measure, noticing a negative shift due to a medication reaction is rarely a clear-cut observation.

It took an entire year after that experience before I was open to trying medication again. At this point, I was back at home, and a year into changing my life, when I decided to act on the advice of my counselor (as stated above in misconception #2).

This time I chose duloxetine (Cymbalta), which lies under the category of SNRI's. As the end of the first month approached, I wasn't experiencing the extreme adverse side effects I'd had with Celexa, which was encouraging, but I also wasn't feeling a major benefit either.

The main side effect I experienced while on Cymbalta was irregular energy levels. I found it hard to get into a consistent sleeping schedule, and I was often tired or wired at the wrong times. There were mornings where I felt like an extra on *The Walking Dead*, dragging my feet just to get to my 10 a.m. class. If I made it through my school day awake, I barely had enough energy to get to the gym, go to work, or start my assignments. Then, the polar opposite would happen at night where I'd feel more wired than usual. It was like I'd been launched from one of those adrenaline-inducing, SlingShot rides that send you flying through the air like a human pebble. I'd be wide-awake at midnight, tossing and turning, unable to shut down and fall asleep. On my doctor's suggestion, I tried taking the medicine at different times, but I still ran into the same problem regardless of any change. I was never able to regulate my energy levels or my sleeping patterns.

The second and less prominent side effect was a feeling of "unnatural suppressed emotion." While I wasn't dealing with major Depression and Anxiety, I noticed that some of my emotions felt limited, mostly with natural reactions like crying. For example, I would watch a movie like *Marley and Me* and know I was supposed to feel sad, or maybe even cry, but it was like the medication unnaturally blocked my ability to do so. I mean come on, if you can watch *Marley and Me* and not tear up, then something's a little off! Some medications, like Zoloft, are notoriously known for this side effect, but on an even more magnified level.

After a year of taking Cymbalta, I did see a positive change. The way I felt on day 365 was much more stable, healthy, and confident than how I felt on day 1. However, I was still making all of the other "moves" I suggest in this book, and therefore, it's hard to say if medication alone was responsible for the positive change. *Personally*, I feel that the other approaches offered in this book are equally as strong "moves" against Depression and Anxiety.

———————————

After my year on medication, I decided to slowly wean off Cymbalta (another important process to monitor with a physician and family supervision). I haven't been on an antidepressant since, and I feel really good. I like knowing that the emotions I'm feeling are natural rather than regulated. I've learned that once you get to a certain point of healing, emotions are actually an indispensable warning signal. Your emotions are like the "check engine light" on your car's dashboard.[1] If you're feeling "off", "down", "worried", or "restless", it's probably being prompted by something. It could be an unchecked habit, a conflict, or a fear or worry that you need to address to shift your feelings. Initiating emotional reflection allows us to make necessary changes to move to a better mental state.

We live in an overmedicated society. (The total number of prescriptions has increased by 85% over the past two decades.[2]) That being said, for some people antidepressants can make a vast improvement in their situation. Do your due diligence with research, and a physician's input, to find the best approach for you.

SUPPLEMENTS

Outside of antidepressants, there is a wide range of supplements that can help alleviate Depression and Anxiety through a more holistic approach. I've found certain supplements to be a helpful addition to my healing process. Listed below are some of the more popular supplements suggested for Depression and Anxiety:

5-HTP: A precursor to serotonin. It supports the production of serotonin by supplying a link to the body's natural production process.

SAM-e: A chemical found naturally in the body. Researchers believe that it may alter the function of different receptors and structures that transport neurotransmitters in the brain. The molecule may also be directly involved in the creation of neurotransmitters.

Saint John's Wort: An herbal supplement. The active ingredients appear to increase the levels of chemical messengers in the brain, such as serotonin, dopamine, and noradrenaline.

These three supplements show promising results when it comes to alternatives for antidepressants.

Know that supplements can cause side effects, especially if taken in high quantities or in conjunction with antidepressants. Approach these options with *professional guidance* and *research* as well.

OTHER SUPPLEMENTS

Probiotics: These are the billions of *good* bacteria in our body. These bacteria help digestion, manufacture certain vitamins, and strengthen the immune system. The gut produces many neurotransmitters, and probiotics help ensure that our bodies have enough good bacteria to produce those neurotransmitters (serotonin, acetylcholine, etc.). Then, those neurotransmitters transition to the brain through the "brain-gut axis." In my opinion, probiotics are a must, especially if you are just starting to change an unhealthy diet. Besides probiotic pills, try drinking Kombucha and diluted

Apple Cider Vinegar drinks as highly beneficial liquids for reducing inflammation and improving gut health.

Omega-3 Fatty Acids: Essential fatty acids that the body needs to function. Omega 3s are important for neurological development and growth, as well as heart health.

B Vitamins: B-12, B-6, and folic acid are significant vitamins that replenish energy levels.

Vitamin D: The vitamin we get from the sun and select foods. Vitamin D levels are often low or lacking in people facing Depression.[3]

Magnesium: A magnesium deficiency is correlated with high levels of stress. It's estimated that up to 75% of people are deficient in magnesium. Magnesium functions in over 300 biochemical reactions throughout the body and can help people feel calmer.[4]

GABA: This produces a relaxing effect by interacting with parts of the nervous system. It can relieve nervous tension, promote relaxation, and has a calming effect after absorption.

Melatonin: This is designed to help you regulate the timing of your sleep, but it doesn't participate in the generation of sleep itself.

Chamomile (and other herbal teas): Herbal teas can provide essential nutrients and antioxidants for the body. Specifically, chamomile is calming and can help improve sleep quality.

Each person's success with supplements varies, similarly to how people react differently to antidepressants. Since I'm not currently on an antidepressant, I find value in consistently taking supplements paired with good nutritional habits. I've taken all of the supplements on the list above at one point or another. Now, I regularly take probiotics, Omega 3s, vitamin D, magnesium, and B-vitamins. Of course, one chapter cannot fully describe all the medicinal measures people can take to see improvement. Other options, like the Genomind test, can predict your specific reaction to a medication. Holistic approaches such as essential oils, acupuncture, and light therapy can be explored as well.

TAKEAWAYS

- Numerous misconceptions exist about taking antidepressants. Be sure that your perception of medication is accurate and fair.
- Antidepressants work well for some people and not as well for others. The same can be said about supplements. Err on the side of caution if you act in this area of healing.
- Always seek professional advice and guidance in this area of *finding better*.

EXHAUSTED PIGEONS

· SLEEP ·

I'm not an early bird or a night owl...
I'm some sort of permanently exhausted pigeon.
-Anonymous

Time for honesty. When it comes to getting good sleep, I'm a work in progress. After three years of pursuing *better* in my own life, this one area is consistently the most challenging for me to manage. I wish I could say that I've mastered finding quality sleep, but I haven't. Waking up for me is a daily battle. Have I tried everything under the sun? Pretty much! Most mornings I find myself hitting the snooze button four to five times before I can even acknowledge that the world is real again! I've tried a sleep study to figure out my habits. I've tried math alarms that require solving equations to turn them off. I've even tried pouring water on my face first thing in the morning to help me roll out of bed. I wish I could say that every night I fall asleep by reading a book nestled in bed, but many times, it's while watching Netflix. Not to mention, my creativity strikes at night. Starting around 8 p.m. and lasting until 1 to 2 a.m., my ability to work creatively skyrockets. Instead of trying to go against my natural wiring, I have learned to lean into this reality, making the most of these productive hours. In fact, much of this book was written in the late hours of the night. This doesn't help me when I need to wake up early to work out, go to a meeting, or take a business call, but it's my genetic makeup. I often beat myself up that I'm not the person who wakes up at 5:30 a.m., ready to go and tackle the world, but I'm working on finding more balance and *finding better* in this area of my life.

This chapter contains sleep research discovered by sleep science professionals. Matthew Walker, director of UC Berkeley's Center for Sleep, and his team have published findings about achieving quality sleep. I've found these suggestions helpful when I'm intentional about applying them to my life.

Sleep is one of the final pieces of the puzzle when approaching Depression and Anxiety through a holistic lens. The suggested nightly sleep amount for young adults is between 7-9 hours of sleep; that's the sweet spot.[1] Anything less can lead to increased stress, decreased job performance, and negative effects on our mind and body.

I found it interesting that our body's natural urge to sleep changes at different ages. If you've been trying to mold yourself into a morning person with no luck (like I have), or can't stay up late to socialize while others can, this could be why:

> "There is [sleep habit] variability from one individual to the next, and that is genetically predetermined. It's called your chronotype. Another way of saying this is that you may be an owl, or you may be a lark. You may be someone who likes to stay up late and then wake up later in the morning. If that's the case, you would be an owl. And the lark—the opposite—they're the early risers, and they are the early-to-bed people. Approximately, 30 percent of the population is one of these two extremes. And then the rest of us sort of sit somewhere in the middle."[5] – M.W.

Regardless of when you choose to go to bed, or what your work-life balance permits in regard to forming a sleep schedule, you can improve sleep quality. Paraphrased, here are Matthew Walker's top five tips.[3]

TOP FIVE TIPS FOR BETTER SLEEP:

- **Create a Dark Environment:** Stay away from phone screens and laptops an hour before going to bed. Screen brightness messes with our circadian rhythm.

- **Practice Regularity:** Go to bed at the same time, and wake up at the same time. Your body needs a sleep routine.

- **Change the Temperature:** Keep it cool at night (65°–68°). A drop in temperature initiates our bodies to fall asleep.

- **Develop Brain Connections:** Teach your brain to connect sleeping with your bed. If you're going to stay awake, do so in another room.

- **Avoid too Much Caffeine or Alcohol:** Try not to drink caffeine after 1 p.m., and never go to bed tipsy. Alcohol can block important cycles of REM sleep.

Realize that sleep is much more critical than just being a part of our daily routine. "Sleep is like a sewage system for your brain—it cleans all the toxins and debris out of your brain. The evidence is resoundingly clear—cutting on sleep makes you less productive and less creative and less effective."[4]

Routinely sleeping less than six or seven hours a night demolishes your immune system, more than doubling your risk of cancer.[5] And with that, consistently sleeping "five hours per night makes you 200-300% more likely to catch a cold than someone sleeping eight hours a night. There isn't any system within your body, or process within the brain that isn't wonderfully enhanced by sleep when you get it, or demonstrably impaired when you don't get enough."[6]

Matthew Walker concludes, "You could be *a far better version of yourself* mentally, cognitively, physiologically if you just got more sleep. "[7]

All of this talk about sleep is leaving out the important concept of rest. While the two go hand in hand, *rest* is different than *sleep*.

While writing this book, I went through a period of burning the candle at both ends. I was not only leaning into my tendency to stay up late, but I was habitually pushing each night to the limit to get this book finished. I was jeopardizing my *rest*.

Finding better takes more than getting sleep; it requires *rest*. *Rest* is taking time to fully recharge so that you can continue to live healthily and balanced. It's taking a break from work, focusing on something else, and being okay with pausing goals.

It's making time for the things that are life-giving to you. *Rest* is investing in that which fills you up.

So, get your *sleep*… but also get your *rest*.

Finding better depends on it.

TAKEAWAYS

- Sleep is often overlooked and undervalued when it comes to the essential restorative effect it has on our mind and body.
- It's suggested that young adults get 7-9 hours of sleep each night.
- To capitalize on the benefits of quality sleep, make sure you practice healthy sleep habits.
- There's *sleep…* and then there's *rest. Rest* is taking a break from goals, expectations, pressure, and busyness. It's setting aside time to recharge. *Rest* is a *must* to *find better.*

PART IV
THE SOUL

A FOREWARD TO FAITH

· THE SOUL ·

The soul becomes dyed with the color of its thoughts.
- Marcus Aurelius

Up until this point, we've discussed ways of *finding better* through improving our mind and body. I'll be the first to say that you can effectively conquer Depression and Anxiety through the "moves" we've already discussed. That being said, there's a third component of our life that we still need to address on our path toward *finding better*: the soul.

> ➤ **SOUL:** a person's moral or emotional nature or sense of identity[1]; the part of a person that is not physical and experiences deep feelings and emotions. *Synonyms:* spirit, innermost self, recesses of the heart.[2]

The condition of our mind and body are compromised when we face Depression and Anxiety and furthermore, I believe our soul can be too. So in this section, I'm going to talk about how I address the condition of my soul. I'm going to talk about the faith that I've found and fostered to further help me make it through Depression and Anxiety. I have found much of my new perspective and purpose through what I'm about to share. It has *shaped my approach to life* and has helped me *find better*, so for that reason, I must include it.

This is not a spiritual book; however, this is a spiritual section. I'm not here to tell you what to believe or how to approach the condition of your soul. You don't have to believe the same things that I do.

If reading a spiritual section makes you uncomfortable... skip it. If you already have established beliefs, and you're not interested in my point of view... skip it. If you want to address physical and mental healing first before considering this section, no problem... skip it and return to it later. If you want to share this book with someone, but you're worried about coming off as spiritual, don't overthink it... they can skip this section too. They will read this same foreword and decide for themselves how they want to finish the book.

The unavoidable issue when discussing spiritual topics is that many people have definite opinions about them. Some people are easily *offended* or *irritated* by discussing this subject. In our current culture, sometimes it can feel like having different opinions means we can't associate with each other, which is a shame. The truth is, humans are meant to explore different ideas, opinions, and beliefs in the search for meaning and purpose.

Nevertheless, I can't control the audience of this book. So at the risk of sounding like a broken record, if you have any issue, reservation, hesitation, irritation, opposition, or negative inclination with reading a spiritual section, that's OK. (And yes, I had to use a thesaurus to rack up all those words!)

Merely skip to the last part of the book, PART V: WRAPPING IT UP, and enjoy the end.

———————

I've written this section over and over, trying to get it just right—attempting to accurately describe the faith I have found. I wasn't prepared for such a challenge when I first started crafting this part, but I quickly realized that discussing spiritual topics is not for the faint of heart; it may very well be one of the most difficult tasks any writer can take on.

After too many attempts to count, reworking line after line, I've come to peace with what I've written. I've found peace in the truth that the best I can do when offering faith-based spiritual advice is to (1) share my beliefs, (2) explain why I have those beliefs, and ultimately, (3) describe the positive impact they have had on the trajectory of my story.

As I talk about spiritual topics and the idea that there's a God, I simply cannot answer every question that may come up (I have many unanswered questions myself). And furthermore, I cannot satisfy every reader's reservations. That's why faith is described as "confidence in things we hope for and assurance about what we do not see."[3] There's an aspect of trust that comes with any level of faith we develop in life. But even with my own lingering questions, my experience of living a life with the addition of faith has helped pull me through my lowest season of Depression and Anxiety. It has become "a," *correction, "the" game-changer in my life.

HIGHWAY 34

· IS THERE MORE? ·

Many days I feel weighed down by the stress of this world, allowing it to shape my thoughts and feelings. I'll find myself running the "rat race" in which so many of us easily get trapped. I subtly begin prioritizing an effort to become more *financially successful* and *outwardly driven.* I seek more acknowledgment from those around me, and I casually let the concept of becoming "more known" sneak into my daily pursuits. And because of these heightened priorities, my mental state begins to shift. My emotions and attitude resemble that of an *unanchored boat on choppy waters.* Tiny things start to irritate me, and I lack empathy for others. My lightheartedness is overtaken by seriousness, and my misdirected thoughts block my clarity and creativity.

I find that when I get stuck in this state, I feel incredibly strung out. I never feel good enough or liked enough or notable enough. Sadly, I've noticed so many people stuck in a similar way. We can all get trapped in this mindset at certain points in life, especially as we grow older and the responsibilities of life increase.

When I start feeling this way, I drive to the foothills and into the mountains in search of a perspective change. There's a hilltop in Colorado, right off of Highway 34, that I go to when I need a reminder that life is not only what we see in the media and the external pressures we feel.

This hilltop has become much more than just a viewpoint for me. It has become a consistent place of reflection and restoration.

A short trail leads to an overlook. Once there, you can see the entirety of Grand Lake, CO. Looking to the left, you see the defined peaks of Rocky Mountain National Park. Looking forward, you see three major lakes: Granby Lake, Shadow Mountain Lake, and Grand Lake. Looking farther toward the horizon sits Mount Baldy with its smooth, rounded top. And to the right of all that, you can see log cabins built from Colorado pine, speckled across the mountain hillside. This breathtaking view cannot be accurately described with words (and a panoramic picture falls short as well).

I've stood on top of this hill multiple times over the past few years. I've stood there during crisp evenings, witnessing one of the world's most beautiful sunsets. I've stood there during the first weeks of fall as the aspen leaves begin to change from ordinary green to warming colors of golden yellow, sun-touched orange, and ruby red.

I've stood there in a foot of packed snow, wearing my favorite hoodie, arms pulled in to stay warm.

I've stood there in the pitch-dark of the night looking up at the stars, outshining the city lights that typically overwhelm them.

At multiple points along my journey, this hilltop has become a "pit stop" for my soul to recharge. *I remember* standing there, holding back tears after my first serious breakup. *I remember* standing there after leaving my first year of college, simply trying to get my feet underneath me again. *I remember* being there as I anxiously paced back and forth worrying about launching my first business. *I remember* standing there before publishing my first book as I debated if it was even worthy of being shared. Needless to say, many moments of weakness have been spent on top of this hill. However, for every moment of weakness, there's been a moment of *gratefulness*, *realization*, and *expectancy* that has followed. Sometimes, healing and guidance has come quickly, and other times it's taken months for a hint of revelation. Thankfully, I've been able to stand there and ultimately realize the crucial purpose behind many of the events in my life.

This spot has become the pinnacle place for me to dig up the dirt of my life and expose worries and doubts that have been weighing me down. I'm able to stand there with an assurance that somehow things will work out. They have in my past, and they will in my future.

Ultimately, the restorative peace I find atop that hill comes from the belief in something much bigger than myself. I stand there with the belief that there's a Creator (God) behind this stunning view. As much as it may feel like it's "myself versus a difficult situation,"… that's not the case. I have more support than that. The same God that created this stunning view is the same God that cares about my life and wants to help me through it.

I'll be the first to admit that I don't always feel deeply connected to God. When I'm running in the "rat race," clouded by a pollution of worldly pressures, the belief that there's a God who is for us and not against us can seem fleeting. Yet when I stand on that hill, I feel the resounding reassurance that there's more purpose and meaning behind our planet, and all of us on it. This assurance drowns out the previous noise.

Did you know that astronomers estimate that there are over 100 billion stars in our universe?[1] What's ironic is that many astronomers will openly admit that we only know about 4% of what resides in outer space.[2]

Even with an insane level of unknown that we face in life, as I stand there, the vastness doesn't bother me. I admire all of the *complexity* and *beauty* and disregard the idea that this is all random. I know deep in my heart—deep in my soul—that we all have a purpose that's inspired by something bigger than ourselves.

To have this kind of "faith in God," you have to step back and look at your own life, the lives around you, and everything that's been masterfully created, and believe that yes, there's got to be more to this. That's the exact conclusion I've come to:

None of this is random.
None of this is by mistake.
And…
None of the struggles we face in life were meant to be faced alone.

The mind-blowing fact that no one on Earth is identical seems like the intentional design of a Creator who desires to use our uniqueness to better others and impact our community. I believe God has wonderfully and uniquely made each of us. I believe He has a plan for our lives that is exceedingly better than we could ever imagine on our own. If we trust in Him and let Him be a part of our lives, then we'll witness this incredible path He has in store for each of us.

We were never meant to do "life" by ourselves. We were never meant to look up at the billions of stars and feel unsettled. Contrary to feelings of worry, fear, and uncertainty...

We were meant to live a life with *faith*.

PERFECTLY IMPERFECT

· A BEDROCK ·

Imagine three buckets labeled *"Mind,"* *"Body,"* and *"Soul."* These buckets make up who we are. We choose how to fill up these buckets as we go through life. Each action, conversation, experience, and belief potentially results in filling up at least one. And yet, if we're not attentive, our buckets can leak, drain, and dry up—becoming depleted. This is why the process of "filling up our buckets" is an ongoing one. We are always adding and maintaining these levels to keep them balanced and filled.

I don't know what you believe in, or what your experiences in life have been thus far. I don't know how you've been raised, treated, or loved. Regardless, I believe that going through life with an empty "Soul" bucket, while possible, can be markedly less peaceful and purposeful. In your battle against Depression and Anxiety, filling up your soul could be one of the most pivotal pieces to *finding better*.

The way I fill up my soul is by actively placing my trust—my faith—in the belief that there's a God, and that He has a positive intention for my life. Taking this one step further, my belief in God also results in my belief in Jesus.

The basis behind my core belief is this:

Humans are flawed and imperfect beings, i.e., we hurt people, we're selfish, we prioritize our image and status, we criticize others, and the list goes on. Jesus, God's son, was and is perfect, and willingly died on our behalf to cover our ever-present imperfections that create a relational gap between God's love and us. Because of what Jesus did, God sees us through a *lens of grace*.[1]

> ➢ **GRACE:** unwavering love, unconditional acceptance, and unending forgiveness

Instead of seeing our imperfections, He sees us as *perfectly imperfect*—covered by His love and acceptance. We can walk in this freeing truth as we pursue becoming a better version of ourselves.

People say that "God is love." That's not wrong.[2] God embodies love and wholeheartedly loves you and me. But, that statement is correct because of what Jesus did on the cross.

———

Speaker and author Carl Lentz simplifies this by saying, "Not only do I believe in God, I believe God created me, Jesus saved me, and His hand continues to guide me regardless of my 'performance' in this life."

I feel the same way.

———————————

Building a relationship with Jesus (which I know sounds weird as I say it) can radically change your perspective on seasons of struggle. It can refocus your approach to life and shift where you find value. And maybe most importantly, knowing Jesus, and trusting in Him, can change your soul. This relationship can free you from feelings like shame, inadequacy, and self-contempt (powerful emotions I've felt before) to open up new purpose and perspective in your life.

When I say the word "relationship," all I mean is the choice to put your trust in Jesus—leaning into faith. It's not complicated like many misperceive. Some people confuse the word "relationship" with the word "religion." The word "religion" can create a false connotation that a life lived with Jesus is a life that requires meeting a spiritual checklist. Do this and don't do that. Add up your rights and wrongs, and then, put them into a formula to see if you passed the test. Some people live this way, basing their worth on their spiritual performance or diligence. The reality is that there's no room for this type of approach in a relationship with Jesus.

A relationship with Jesus is personal. It's based on acceptance and love—two characteristics that perfectly define Him. He just wants to know you and to guide your life—being a model to mirror after. Sure, our world and our personal lives still need rules and checklists. There are still repercussions for our decisions. We need to strive to be good people—to seek the change we hope to see. But, when Jesus enters the picture, the expectation to meet a spiritual standard is removed.

Freeing, isn't it?

I lean on Jesus in times of struggle and in times of triumph. I pray (I'll explain my approach to prayer later) when I feel a need for guidance and clarity. And, I let Jesus define who I am—*perfectly imperfect*—rather than letting my life be defined by my failures or insecurities. I know deep in my soul what Jesus thinks and says about me, which is what I hope to share in the following chapter because it's the same way He feels about you. And since I've put my faith in God/Jesus as the major component behind my life's path, how He feels about me is really all that matters.

This *bedrock of faith* I'm describing offers more love, hope, and purpose.

And regarding Depression and Anxiety, you better believe that having this *bedrock of faith* helps me get through the low seasons until I make it to the high ones.

For any reader who has never fully understood Jesus, this all might seem perplexing.

How can "Jesus" actually factor into me finding better?

That's where we're headed next...

FACTS ONLY

· A BEDROCK (CONT.) ·

From what's recorded in the Bible, Jesus embodied *judgment-free love*. He went out of his way to encourage and help the less fortunate. He never withheld relationship and connection. He interacted with all kinds of people, from the presumptuous, wayward leaders, to the sick and lonely.

There's an account of this *judgment-free* love in the Bible that depicts his character:

Jesus had been traveling from one village to another, and on the way, he stopped at a Samaritan village for water. When he reached the village well, he encountered a woman drawing water. From her outward appearance and demeanor, the woman appeared to be emotionally fragile and outcast. In fact, she was at the well mid-day in the intense afternoon heat because it was the only time she could go to avoid the judgment and mistreatment she usually received from others.

Paraphrased, this was their conversation[1] ...

Jesus asked her, *"May I have some water?"*

Shocked she replied, *"Why are you willing to talk to me? Do you know who I am?"* ...

(A little bit of context) In this period of time, their conversation broke all religious and social discriminatory boundaries. For one, their differing religious backgrounds discouraged them from associating with each other. Secondly, she was a woman. The imbalance of rights and respect, while still present in our culture today, was unimaginably unequal at that time in history. Women were looked down upon and endured continual disrespect from men. Thirdly, like some of us, she felt defined by her messy past. Her life was riddled with unhealthy relationships, and the events of her past placed her at the bottom of the social rung of the village. Likely, she was feeling shame and regret — Depression and distress. She couldn't comprehend why this man was not only talking to her, but also treating her with respect and kindness.

The conversation between Jesus and the woman continued...

She reiterated, *"If you knew me, if you knew what I've done, then you wouldn't want to talk to me."*

He calmly replied, *"I know exactly who you are."* (I mean this is the Son of God we're talking about. Surely, He knows people well. But, she didn't realize that yet.)

He continued to affirm her by saying, *"If you knew who I truly was, then you'd want much more than just the water from this well."*

Intrigued by His response, she asked, *"Are you the Son of God? The one people have been talking about?"*

He replied, *"Yes. I come to offer more than just water. I come to offer a full life. A life filled with love, hope, and grace to those who get to know me."*

The story doesn't offer more details about the woman's life thereafter, but it's presumed that she left that conversation with a peace that she'd never felt before. She went on to share her experience of encountering Jesus with others. Not only was she refreshed from drinking the water from the well, but her soul was refreshed from hearing the peaceful words and promise spoken over her by Jesus.

I can only assume that her soul was filled from that encounter; very similar to when a coworker speaks highly of us on our behalf, or when a close friend acknowledges how special we are to them. Not only did the Son of God take the time to have a conversation with her, but He also gave her positive recognition and affirmation. There's a big difference between just having a "conversation" and actually initiating real "recognition."

Jesus was the original advocate for breaking social injustice, as demonstrated by his desire to start interactions like this one. He stood for equality. He broke all social boundaries to show her that she had *value* and *promise*.

Why is this account of Jesus so important to each of our individual journeys?

The character of God and the character of Jesus are one and the same, so if I'm struggling with Depression and Anxiety, then I need a God who acts in this same way toward me. God sees my struggles and imperfections, and yet, only has *compassion* and *forgiveness* for me like Jesus had for the woman at the well.

Look at the three most used words in the Bible.[2] These words fully embody the character of God/Jesus:

LOVE: Mentioned 551 times
JOY: Mentioned 218 times
GRACE: Mentioned 131 times

Don't you think our world (and our personal battle with Depression and Anxiety) needs more *love, joy,* and *grace?* Just watch the news for five minutes, and you'll be quickly reminded of this.

The more you begin to discover the character of God, the more you begin to realize the lens through which He views us. No matter how low we feel about ourselves, we have a Creator who looks at us through a *lens of grace.* He loves us for who we are, not for who we think we should be. He wants us to recognize that the shame we may feel from decisions or choices in our past doesn't hold any power over our future. What we've negatively said, done, or felt toward others and ourselves is not what defines our current worth or our future potential. He wants nothing but the best for you and me, and He will relentlessly approach us from a posture of grace to achieve this. Amidst all the challenges we face in this lifetime, this truth is liberating.

———————————

Many people believe that their lifestyle isn't endorsed by the Bible, so why build a "relationship" with Jesus? The truth is that God isn't concerned about the perfection of your heart, but rather, the direction of your heart. As Carl Lentz says, "Faith in God isn't behavioral modification, but spiritual transformation." There's a massive difference between the two. When your soul heals, you naturally make changes in your life for the better.

If someone says you can't receive love or grace from God because of XYZ, then they're not speaking the truth. If you've heard that God only has an attitude of judgment, then you're listening to the wrong source. If you've been hurt by a person claiming to know God and living a life of faith, then understand that their actions are part of the flawed human nature, not the character of God.

Likewise, when certain religious people claim that others are separated from the ability to have a real, genuine relationship with Jesus because of certain aspects of their identity (e.g., sexual orientation, gender identity, or any other distinct human uniqueness), then they're radically misunderstanding and underestimating the love and acceptance Jesus clearly says He offers. Furthermore, they're incredibly undermining who Jesus is, the way in which He unrestrictedly loves people, and the intentional significance and impact behind what He chose to do while here on earth.

He doesn't say some of us are broken, and some of us are not. We all are broken, imperfect people that God chooses to cover in redeeming love (that's the Bible in one sentence).[3]

#PerfectlyImperfect

He doesn't say:

- If you're considered popular by your peers, then He'll love you
- If you have thousands of Instagram followers, then He'll love you
- If you've only had heterosexual relationships, then He'll love you
- If you've never been divorced, then He'll love you
- If you've never used drugs, then He'll love you
- If you've never missed church, then He'll love you
- If you've never discriminated against another person, then He'll love you.
- If you've never had suicidal thoughts, then He'll love you.

FACTS ONLY: He loves you for who you truly are. *He knows* everything about you. *He knows* how many hairs are on your head. *He knows* that none of what you're going through is easy. *He knows* that you're *tired* and *at the end of your rope.* And... *He knows* that without a doubt you'll get through this season of Depression and Anxiety to become a more impactful person *cloaked in discernment* and *empowered by compassion.*

And furthermore, *He knows* the dreams you have in your heart: to start that business, to write that book, to meet that person, to get the promotion, to make the team, to finish the degree, and to find your calling.

Gone are the things of the past; He wants to do new things in your life, *making a way through the wilderness.*

This is the God of Love.
This is the God of Joy.
This is the God of Grace.

This... is the God I know.

TAKEAWAYS

- Faith is the belief in something bigger than ourselves. One step further, faith in God is the belief that we're fully loved, ALWAYS covered in grace, and empowered to live with joy as we work through our pain.
- God embodies inclusion, not exclusion.
- A relationship with Jesus starts the second you say, "Jesus, I'm imperfect. I want the freedom, peace, and perspective you offer. I believe." It doesn't start when you accomplish a certain level of perfection or standard. That's what makes this kind of faith so special.

*Check out Lauren Daigle's song "You Say" as a perfect representation of these takeaways.[4]

A MOMENT OF SILENCE

· PRAYER/MEDITATION ·

Every night of my freshman year of college, I'd pray before going to bed. At this point in my life, the idea of prayer was a newer concept to me. While I had grown up in a family that prayed, I rarely attempted to participate. It wasn't until I started to struggle that I decided to explore faith-backed prayer as a part of my healing. I can vividly remember my prayer routine each night. I didn't have some sort of prayer template, and many times I felt like I was mindlessly relaying lottery-like requests to an "invisible" God. I would lay in bed and silently ask for complete healing. Yes, it seemed like a long-shot, and quite frankly a desperate request, but I was broken and willing to try. It was worth believing my prayers might be answered, and that I'd wake up with a new mind, body, and spirit—and my self-confidence restored.

I'd pray something like this:

> God… if you're real, then you have the
> power to heal. I'm asking that you heal my
> acne. May I please wake up with clearer
> skin? I'm asking that you help redirect my
> thoughts. May I please wake up happier? I'm
> asking that you heal my loneliness and
> sadness. I miss my family, friends, and
> girlfriend. May I please wake up with more
> peace over those relationships? God, it seems
> like my friends at other colleges are having a
> better time than me. Why do I feel so down?
> Why do I feel so lost? Why do I feel so
> broken? I'm asking that you help redirect
> these feelings. May I wake up with new
> energy and confidence?

Sometimes, the promises that God says he'll
carry out in our lives seem unrealistic. The Bible
includes promise after promise that God says He
will fulfill.[1] Trust me, many nights (almost every
night), I wrestled with the idea that a "God," that no
one can see or hear, would actively move in my life
to heal me. Every day, I had the choice to let go or
hold on to my newfound faith that He did have a
greater plan for my life.

One of His promises is, "If you ask, then you will receive."[2] What a simple, yet profound promise. I took the reassurance behind that statement into my prayers every night, asking for healing and peace in all areas of my life — trusting that there was some sort of good to be found around the corner.

If prayer is something that you've never tried, or maybe the idea of it completely turns you off, I'm here to let you know that you're not alone. Below is my take on prayer. It's what I've found to be true over the last few years of my life. I hope these thoughts will bring you some new clarity.

THOUGHTS ON PRAYER

Similar to meditation, a part of prayer is taking time to pause negative thoughts that are spinning out of control and seek grounding; it's a conscious choice to release them. If you don't have a simple way of doing so, your battle with Depression and Anxiety can feel non-stop.

———————

Prayer is letting emotions fly at a God who says He can handle our anger, frustration, and pain. Many people think that if they pray, then their prayers must be polite and perfected. It would seem foolish to speak to God in a tone of dissatisfaction. I mean you kind of want to be on the good side of the

Creator of the Universe, right? But, this is a misconception. *Prayer is a form of communication.* When have you ever communicated with another person consistently and not let emotions drive the conversation? It's about being *real*, not *righteous*.[3] Be honest and authentic. He can handle it... and He wants to.

Prayer doesn't have to be a long, drawn-out process. While many people may find stability in a consistent routine, i.e., praying to start one's morning, journaling after prayer, etc., it's not a requirement. Don't mistake this as me saying there's no value and purpose in longer, intentional periods of prayer. However, prayer is not some spiritual equation, where the more time you spend praying, the more God will love you and act in your life to bless your endeavors. It's not like God is sitting up in Heaven with a stopwatch timing our efforts, and after 30 minutes of prayer or 3,750 spoken words (whichever comes first), we're then "granted" a good day. His love is never based on performance. Therefore, I'm a big believer in the power behind simple, short prayers. These are the 30 second "game time" moment prayers, where you acknowledge the situation and the opportunity that comes with it.

Such as…

- before an interview
- before a game
- before a work shift
- before a date
- before a confrontation
- before a phone call
- before a prognosis

…all moments where nervous thoughts based on uncertainty and doubt can run rampant in our hearts and minds.

I typically pray something like this:

> "God, first of all, thank you. Thank you for this opportunity. Thank you for this moment. Thank you for XYZ. I pray that you go before me. I pray that you give me the confidence and capability to perform at my best. I pray for peace despite any fear I may feel. And no matter what, I trust the outcome knowing that I gave it my all. Help me to trust you with whatever happens. I'm certain that you know what's best/next for me in your plan over my life. Here we go… let's own this moment.

Just like that, you've armored yourself with 30-seconds of powerful prayer. While it may seem short, it's actually the foundation that grounds you before any situation. It's no longer about you vs. the world, but something much more surmountable.

Prayer isn't an audible, two-way conversation between you and God (or at least not in my experience). The statement, "I heard from God" usually weirds people out. For nineteen years, I irritably took this phrase literally, and therefore, consistently avoided prayer. I pictured religious people praying to God and then hearing a deep-voiced response, like the narrator of *The Deadliest Catch*.

After three years of prayer being a part of my life, I've never audibly "heard" God's voice. I've realized that God "speaks" to us in many ways beyond what we would consider traditional communication. He will purposefully use people, books, podcasts, and other mediums to "speak" influence into our lives. There are moments where specific conversations stand out because of their profound impact on our individual journey. If God promises to work through you to make a difference in other people's lives, then you can bet that the same is true for the people he's put in your life that have become *beacons of encouragement* and *direction*.

When I feel like He's *directly* speaking to me, I usually notice a stirring in my heart. I'll get a slight "gut-feeling" or an emotional response that guides me in a new direction or encourages me to seek a fresh perspective. I feel a nudge to take a step in a certain area of my life. Or, the subtle reassurance that it will all work out. Or, the gentle push to make amends with someone. Or, the hopeful reminder to be patient, but also expectant. These are the faint feelings that I "hear" from God. Many people may call this just human intuition, but I stand to question that. I've lived a majority of my life by my own "intuition," and all it got me was trouble, heartache, or misdirection.

It's up to you and me to pray for, and then act on, these gentle nudges. Then, it comes down to *trusting* that He will go before us, providing the right resources and guidance required for our unique plan.

And that's exactly what He did in my story. It just didn't look like I thought it would.

In the next chapter, I'll share what I mean…

TAKEAWAYS

- Prayer should be treated like *normal, consistent* communication rather than *timid, contrived* interaction.
- Prayer (similar to meditation) is taking a moment to lift up worry and find thankfulness during your current season of life.
- "Hearing" from God comes in many forms. It could be a meaningful word that pops into your head, a promising verse or quote, an impactful mentor, a stirring of the heart, or a prompting to find a new perspective, all of which could be important catalysts for your journey.

WHY DID THIS HAPPEN TO ME?

· TOUGH QUESTIONS ·

When we think of the possibility and existence of God, the question that usually arises is: *If God is real, if He is good, if He is supposed to protect and strengthen me, then why is this happening in my life? If God is for me and not against me, then why do I feel this way?*

Have you ever had any of these thoughts?

Even if faith isn't a part of your life, most certainly you've had these questions surrounding God. It seems to be a very common barrier between having faith and disputing the existence of God.

Honestly, it's a valid question.

When I was going through my lowest season, questions like the ones above usually outweighed a positive perspective on God. I consistently felt disappointed that I wasn't receiving any help. I felt hopeless, sincerely believing that I'd never feel better. Sometimes I was even straight-up angry with this "loving" God that seemed to be leaving my life untouched.

As I said in the last chapter...
- I prayed for my severe acne to clear up.
- I prayed for the constant heavy thoughts to disappear.
- I prayed for my Anxiety to settle.
- And, I prayed for my life to change for the better.

How many of those prayers were answered by God during my first year of college?

A BIG WHOPPING ZERO!

Ironically, I felt like my life actually took a turn for the worse. Just when I started to have a strong faith in God, my life spiraled downward at an alarming rate. I ended up at rock bottom, having one persistent thought, "I want to be done with this life."

What I didn't know then, but I recognize now, is that God *was* working in my life. He was *protecting, healing,* and *guiding* me the entire time. What many of us don't understand is that while we're going through life's toughest seasons, God's plan rarely matches our idea of what we think is the "best" plan for our life. We question the validity of faith when things don't go the way *we* had hoped.

If I could have had it my way, my prayers would have been answered under my timeline. I would have been healed right then and there. There would have been no need to leave my out-of-state college to come back to Colorado, initiating an intense healing process. That was *my* "Plan A"... I didn't have a "Plan B." However, what would my plan have resulted in?

If I would have healed on my timeline, sure, I may have looked better (acne free) and felt immediate relief from negative thoughts, but my character would have stayed the same. I wouldn't have engaged in the year of intense "self-work" it took for me to *find better*. Without a change in character, my habits would have also stayed the same. My values in life would have never shifted. While I may have had my prayers answered that first year of college, my story would have looked completely different.

Here's what my timeline probably would have resulted in:

I'd still be living out of state, not quite finished with school, and most likely starting to look for a job there. I probably would have settled for taking a marketing job with a company that I had little interest in, rather than exploring meaningful projects like this one.

I'd likely still be a low-grade alcoholic, covering up my habits with the excuse that it's part of the 20-something culture. I would have continued to believe that drinking regularly and heavily wasn't harmful to my mind, body, and personal success. I would have continued to lean on partying/drinking as my main source of fun and a primary determinant of my identity.

I'd have friends that were entertaining to be around, but maybe not the best group of people to associate with to become a better version of myself.

I'd be less selective with dating, allowing sexually-driven relationships to be a major filler in my life. I would have been carelessly involved with people, even if they were toxic to me (or just not in it for the long haul). All of this would have further perpetuated my deep-seated insecurities.

And the life I would have lived goes on...

See what I mean?! I would have been living my idea of a "normal life," but actually selling myself short of much greater potential.

Here's what actually happened:

Broken, I came home.

My desperate desire to clear up my skin led me to find a holistic esthetician/nutritionist in Colorado.[1] Shout out to you Jesse! The program she put me on, while strictly regimented, stirred my desire to explore health and wellness in all areas of my life.

I began to exercise regularly. My love for working out sparked the idea of becoming a personal trainer. I became certified and began working at a corporate gym in less than six months. After some time there, my entrepreneurial spirit kicked in. I opened my first personal training studio in the garage of my aunt's house. While learning the ins and outs of running a business, I attended my new school, University of Colorado–Denver. Because of the UCD's diverse program offerings, I was able to increase my credit load and finish college in three years. Equipped with a degree in marketing and some initial success with my first business, I stepped it up a notch and opened a training studio in downtown Denver. I built a varied clientele base that even included professional actors from the Denver Center for the Performing Arts.

Over this time, I diligently invested in counseling. (Or should I say, my counselor invested in me!) I changed the habits that were impeding my life. I put myself into my own "self-induced rehabilitation," and I stopped drinking altogether. I realized it was magnifying my Depression and Anxiety, and altering my authenticity.

The time at home allowed me to strengthen my relationships with my family. Specifically, my relationship with my father shifted from being tense and rocky, to loving and respectful. He's quickly become one of my best friends and closest confidants—someone I can only hope to model my life after.

And finally, I found Red Rocks Church. I had never attended a place where EVERYONE was fully accepted. A place where love is practiced and kindness abounds. A church where the pastors proudly wear tall-tees paired with skinny jeans and two-toned Air Max '90s. They openly talk about their struggles in hopes to better connect with people... and it works! I've found lifelong friends there that encourage me to be the most successful, grounded person I can be. And... my belief that there's a God has been countlessly reassured.

Everything included in this book has been a result of those few years. So YEAH, looking back, I'm glad God led me through His timeline and not mine! If not, my life would have been much more empty and incomplete. My "Plan A" was a surefire path to mediocrity. "Plan B"—led by God's timeline—resulted in the life I have today. It required a drawn-out, demanding process of *finding better*, but that developed me into the person I believe God intended me to be. That's the incredible thing about God's hand on our lives. He can take a horrible situation and turn it around to positively impact our life story. I know He never intended for me to struggle as much as I did during my lowest season of Depression and Anxiety—that wasn't His doing, but rather the compounding of my *own* lifestyle decisions and habits. However, I do believe that once I put my faith in Him and asked Him to "step in and help pull me out of it," He guided me down the only path which could actually turn things around—one that molded me into a better person. This is where the "ask and you shall receive" promise comes in to play. When we trust in God and ask Him to move in our lives… He does. But, it's not always in a way we had *pictured*, or at a *pace* we had wanted, or along a *path* that we could have imagined. He can take our mess—or our pain—and bring good from it.

All along the way, I trusted in Him, praying to know what steps I should take next. I continued to pray for healing, which did eventually come. And going forward, I'm still expectant that He can continue to use my story for good.

What about your life? Are you asking God to act on your timeline?

In our current culture of having things immediately delivered to us, it may seem cruel to have to "wait" on God to move in our lives.

However, He's not waiting, rather, He's working behind the scenes. Having patience through pain can have a purpose. Two years from now, where will He have you? If you let Him lead, your life will be significantly crafted with more passion and purpose.

DISCLAIMER: Don't mistake my testimony as a suggestion to sit back and let Him do all the work.

Work *with* God to *find better*.

Speaker and author, Mark Batterson, puts it this way, "Pray like it all depends on God. Work like it all depends on you."

Let God work behind the scenes as you work in the present. Pray for strength and discernment as you walk in a new direction. Pray for a sound mind that's enabled by a faith-driven perspective. Pray for powerful courage that's humbly expressed. Pray for the daily emotional posture to love others well. Pray that you can stay true to the process of *finding better*.

You might not be able to see the whole picture right now, but we never really can. The best we can do is show up in faith knowing that hindsight will undoubtedly be 20/20.

TAKEAWAYS

- God's timeline rarely matches ours.
- God's working behind the scenes of your life and going before you in everything you do.
- Many times, our "Plan A" fails. What we had hoped for or envisioned falls apart. However, God can take what feels like a "Plan B," and turn it into something incredible—something that's better than our "Plan A" could have ever been.

P.S.

I never thought I would write a book, much less a bold section on faith. But, it's a thing now.

Faith really has impacted my journey, and I'd be lying if I didn't believe that it could change yours.

At some point, all of us have to process our understanding of this world and matters related to the soul. We each choose how we respond to these tough questions. Faith is what I choose. (At least, on most days!)

I say most days, because the truth is, some days my faith feels stronger than others. And, I'm totally okay with that. In fact, I think it's normal.

Are there times when I doubt the whole "Jesus" thing?
YUP

Are there days where I don't feel my prayers matter?
MANY

Are there moments where I wonder if putting my energy into faith is worth it?
OF COURSE

Are there times where I feel like certain Christians don't represent faith well?
YES

Are there weird Christians that make me question my stance on faith?

ABSOLUTELY

…Standing on college campuses and shouting religious jargon for example. Like what the heck. Nobody wants that! I've chalked it up to one simple truth: There are weird people EVERYWHERE— Christians and non-Christians alike! The world is a mixed bag. The moral of the story: Don't be a weird person.

Was I nervous to share my beliefs on faith?
YES… and NO

The fact is that faith is bold. Spiritual concepts are not tangible like most things we experience. Exploring spiritual topics requires depth to the approach. If you've ever seen a 3D graph, faith is neither the X nor the Y-axis but the Z. I believe living life with this "three-axis perspective" is a choice.

I hope this section made you think. I hope it brought encouragement in a way you didn't expect. In a way, I hope it has helped make faith more "tangible."

And even if not… that's okay.

PART V

WRAPPING IT ALL UP

WHO'D YOU VOTE FOR?

· FORMING HABITS ·

What happens if you read each chapter in this book and act on each "move" only once?

- You go to the gym… once.
- You choose to eat healthily… once.
- You meet with a counselor… once.
- You try managing your thoughts… once.
- And every other possible "move" you could make, you try… once.

What will happen? Will your life radically change overnight, "sling-shotting" you toward immediate health and wellness to beat Depression and Anxiety?

The answer: No

What if you try making moves in the right direction for a week? Will that be enough to come out on the other side?

The answer: No

What about a month?

The answer: Better, but still... No.

This is the point in the book where people feel an inner confliction and hear a voice raising the questions; *Do I really have what it takes to become a better version of myself? Do I want to fight for this? Is it worth the effort?*

The conclusion I hope you come to is...

Yes. Yes, it is!

Each chapter before this one has laid out a specific "move" you can make against Depression and Anxiety. However, unless you act on those "moves" over and over again, with intentional consistency, then *finding better* will just be some *wishful outcome* you desire for your life, rather than an *actual outcome.*

That's not what I want for anyone.

I desperately want anyone reading this book to truly *find better.*

To do this though, I have to expand upon what the process is honestly going to take. Nothing about seeking transformation is easy. It takes *continual, dedicated* action. So going forward, I'm not going to hold back. I won't water down describing the mindset you'll need to see a true transformation.

———————

We all know that a consistent action is defined as a "habit." More importantly, *certain habits* can have a *transformative effect* on our life. One of my favorite quotes demonstrating this *transformative effect* is attributed to Mahatma Gandhi:

> "Keep your thoughts positive because your thoughts become YOUR WORDS.
> Keep your words positive because your words become YOUR BEHAVIOR.
> Keep your behavior positive because your behavior becomes YOUR HABITS.
> Keep your habits positive because your habits become YOUR VALUES.
> Keep your values positive because your values become YOUR DESTINY."

The gripping truth is that a habit can be either good or bad. Good habits will place your life on a track toward a higher destination. Bad habits will send you down a track toward a lower destination. The choice is yours.

For example, if a person has a habit of going out drinking every weekend, from a perspective of social habits, they may be defined as a "partier." But let's say they drink at every social outing and even throughout the day just to "relax." They may now be considered an "alcoholic," rather than just a "partier." You see, if we let our bad habits escalate, then we jeopardize the quality of our lives even more.

This same principle of "escalated bad habits" applies to many other actions. Here's another example:

A person's small decision to watch porn every once in a while, turns into the habitual craving to watch porn every day. And while watching porn may be prevalent in our culture, are there any solid facts that watching porn makes us better, more connected humans?[1] Seriously? Or, does it just lead to less satisfaction in our relationships, and an addictive, self-destructive habit that prevents people from finding true intimacy and self-confidence? Yup... I just went there.

Or, what about when a person smokes a JUUL pod once a week, and before they know it, that seemingly harmless act turns into an addictive habit that has them ripping through pods as if they were Capri Suns. When they attempt to go a week without JUULing, they feel notably on edge, anxious, and wired.

Or, what if a person's hobby for playing video games turns into a consuming habit of playing for hours every day. I do believe esports will be one of the biggest phenomena of the next ten years, continuing to grow to be as recognized as other top professional sports. However, if someone is gaming

---

to the extent that it's keeping them from connecting with their inner circle, inhibiting their ability to advance in a separate, more promising career, or interfering with their sleep schedule and physical well-being, then it's a hobby that's escalated to become a bad habit. A gamer can be a "workaholic" too.

Before moving on, it's worth saying again that none of these examples come from a position of prejudice. I've had to face countless bad habits that had me living my life at a lower potential.

Now, let's look at the principle of "escalated good habits," and the result they have on our lives.

Look at something like personal finances. Maybe you make a habit of buying only what you need: spending less on brand name items, GrubHub deliveries, and nonessential tech products. Before you know it, you're saving chunks of cash every week. In a couple of years, this habit has allowed you to save enough money to rent a spacious apartment or make a down payment on a permanent place. People on the outside looking in might label this as financial prosperity, when in reality it's just financial responsibility. This is the potential of implementing good habits in our lives. *If we escalate our good habits, then they further propel us toward a greater outcome.*

Author James Clear, a habit researcher, states: "Every action you take is a vote for the type of person you wish to become. No single instance will transform your beliefs, but as the votes build up, so does the evidence of your new identity."[2]

We hear so much about forming good habits that it often feels redundant. Whether it's setting New Year's Resolutions, S.M.A.R.T. goals, or 5 Year Plans, we get inundated to the point that it can devalue the importance of consistent choice making. We can easily underestimate the effect habits have in our lives and the identity that they develop for us. It's true that every day we're voting for a future version of ourselves. Every time you go to the gym or choose to eat healthily, that's a vote for your new identity. Every time you sit down and study/read/create instead of watching Netflix, that's a vote for your identity. Every time you push past social anxiety and practice good communication, that's another vote for your identity. And before you know it, your new overarching identity becomes someone who's intellectual and well-rounded, able to hold engaging conversations, outwardly fit, and inwardly healthy. Not a bad identity for which to be known!

If we wake up every day knowing that our choices are a crucial vote for the future person we will become, then maybe our actions will seem a bit more important in the moments that we make them.

Hopefully, you're starting to picture a better version of yourself: happier, healthier, focused, and less insecure. Maybe you're visualizing a more confident version of yourself, a version that's comfortable in any situation; a version that's equipped to take on challenges that were once Anxiety-ridden. You're analyzing your current habits, and wondering, *Why have I been selling myself short? I want to start voting on my life differently.*

You're excited.

You're feeling pumped up to make a change!

As a result of my own path to find a better version of myself (and as part of my research for writing this book), I've read many "self-improvement" books. Most of them have a "call to action" chapter similar to the section above. It's a chapter that gets the reader excited to make a change, similar to the way you may be feeling right now. When I read this section in books, I quickly become inspired too! It doesn't matter if it's the venture capitalist trying to motivate business readers, or the World Class athlete trying to rouse the dreams of young athletes, or even the poised life coach trying to build up grit in their dedicated fans. Each writer uses their own unique phrasing to evoke passion in their audience and initiate forward movement.

But, what really happens?

If you're like the majority of humans on planet Earth, then most likely that motivation only carries over into your life briefly. The next day is passionately spent planning improvement strategies, writing down dreams, and setting clear limits on bad habits. For a week, things go well, and then... *life happens*. Things get in the way, heightened motivation dwindles, and you fall off the wagon—SMACK! Any previous bad habits and poor decisions come racing back in, replacing the potential for an extraordinary life and shifting it back to mediocre. This commonly happens without us even realizing it. The truth is, Depression and Anxiety feed off of bad habits. They will take as much ground as you give them. If this common drop-off happens to you, then Depression and Anxiety will likely win.

———————

Why is self-improvement so stinkin' hard? Why is a drop-off the most common outcome? I mean seriously, why is sticking to something, even if we know it's beneficial, ridiculously challenging? What's the force that keeps us from casting consistent votes toward who we want to be?

It's all summed up in one word: Resistance.

Let me explain…

Any vision you have of yourself doing something worthwhile or meaningful will quickly collide head-on with a feeling of "Resistance."

I recently listened to a podcast conversation between author Steven Pressfield and Oprah Winfrey, where they talked about this concept of Resistance.[3] His explanation was so compelling, I felt I needed to share it.

Steven Pressfield defines Resistance as "that negative force that arises whenever we try to move from a lower level to a higher level." Every person who has ever sought to become a better version of themselves faces it. It's like gravity; it's a natural force present in every beneficial decision we might make. It creates internal tension, doubt, fatigue, and thoughts that attempt to persuade *us to do something easier, to aim lower,* or *to give up.*

Steven shared what he believes to be "Resistance's Greatest Hits: A list of those activities that most commonly face Resistance."

RESISTANCE'S GREATEST HITS:
- the launching of any entrepreneurial venture or enterprise
- any diet or health regimen
- any program of spiritual advancement
- any activity whose aim is tighter abdominals

- any course or program designed to overcome an unwholesome habit or addiction
- pursuing education of any kind
- the undertaking of any enterprise or endeavor whose aim is to help others
- any act that entails a commitment of the heart; the decision to get married, to have a child, to weather a rocky patch in a relationship
- the taking of any principled stand in the face of adversity

And if I could add one more specific "Greatest Hit" to his list it would be:
- any "move" made to battle Depression or Anxiety

A general rule of thumb is "the more *important* an activity is, the more Resistance you feel to it." Drawing from my experience, I can't think of many things more *important* than fighting back against Depression and Anxiety each day to promote a healthier, more peaceful version of ourselves.

———

Resistance can feel like many things. It's the negative thoughts that keep us from taking a step forward. It's the feeling that the temporary comfort of settling, or the comfort of seeking distraction and being lazy, is better than actually doing the hard work to see something through. It's the impulse to cover insecurities and pain through a substance, rather than fighting to address those feelings appropriately. It's the feeling that sways us to take a shortcut or the easy way out. It's the feeling convincing us we'll always look/be/act a certain way so we might as well find acceptance, rather than pursuing a life lived above average. It's the voice of comparison, telling us we can't accomplish something to the extent that another person has, so why even try?

The key characteristic to note about Resistance is that it comes after the dream. What happens first is feeling excited about a dream to improve, to innovate, to create, to change. But, Resistance would rather keep you dreaming than actually acting on the dream. Pressfield says that "most of us have two lives: the life we live and the unlived life within us. Between the two, stands Resistance." *MIC DROP

In conjunction with this statement, he shared that he no longer overanalyzes his progress at the end of each day, but instead, he simply asks himself, "Did I overcome Resistance today?" This self-reflecting question pairs perfectly with a habit-based quote that I love from speaker Levi Lusko, who says: "Long-term consistency is better than short-term intensity."

This book is all about changing your identity through *long-term consistency*. It's about beating Depression and Anxiety through many different "moves" that require a determined *lifestyle* change. However, if you dive headfirst into transformation, hoping to sustain overly exhaustive efforts longer than a month, then eventually your tank will empty and the "drop-off" will occur. At the same time, if you don't act with enough intention, and you only half-heartedly attempt to transform, then positive change won't happen either.

There's a *middle ground* between those two extremes where you'll find sustained life-change, and a new, empowered identity. Life is all about engaging in this balancing act. If you genuinely ask yourself, "Did I overcome Resistance today?"... and you did, then I believe you'll elicit the perfect amount of forward movement to develop a better version of yourself. As you take strides forward, Resistance will ALWAYS be present. The common belief that after 21 days, habits shift into autopilot is a myth. There hasn't been a day where I've woken up without feeling some sort of internal Resistance toward accomplishing the goals I've set for myself.

———————

There's no quick fix to overcome Resistance. Realizing it's going to be present and then pushing forward is all that has to happen. One of my all-time favorite mottos comes from Carl Lentz who says, "Own the Moment."[4] It's become my life statement. To "Own the Moment" means to push past Resistance (worry, doubt, hesitancy, or laziness) to take a courageous step forward—owning the moment in front of me to the best of my ability.

All of this being said, when it comes to forming habits, I have to admit that I think my most powerful (and most practiced habit) might sound a bit unusual. The most important habit I have developed is that of getting back up after moments where Depression and Anxiety have knocked me down. I wish nothing more for you than to develop this same habit. It may very well be the most important one of them all.

I'll admit there are still times where Depression and Anxiety steal my confidence or my attention during a conversation. They show up and steal a quiet Tuesday night, and the peace within me. But I never let these moments drag on. I've made a habit of getting back up and into the game. Resistance tries to convince me to *stay down* and live in a state of *less* freedom and *more* fear, but that's where I've made a firm habit to never settle. I've formed a habit to make all the "moves" in this book to get back on track and keep heading toward *better*.

And from this process, I've learned that perfection doesn't exist, but persistence does.

That's the mindset I now live by.

TAKEAWAYS

- Habits can be either good or bad. Your actions really do matter.
- Every chapter in this book can be turned into a good habit. With the right habits in place, Depression and Anxiety have no chance of winning.
- Every day we face feelings of Resistance. But when we face it head-on, and "Own the Moment,"[3] the byproduct is a life where we continually blaze past our previous potential.

THE DEFINITION OF INSANITY

· TIME FOR A CHANGE ·

Sometimes, no matter how hard we have worked to transform ourselves, bigger change is still needed. We can grit our teeth and attempt to push forward, but it may not be the right "move."

What I'm saying is that you may need to uproot and flat-out leave a situation behind you to fully *find better*. I'm not talking about leaving for the morning and heading to a local coffee shop or taking a two-week trip in hopes of resetting. I'm talking about initiating BIG CHANGE. We tend to take on the qualities of our environment; it molds our perspectives and potential. Because of this, our environment (people, places, jobs, etc.) is as much of a factor in our mental health as is our own personal improvement.

For me, one of my "BIG CHANGES" was leaving my out-of-state school to come back to college in Denver. Leaving my original friend group... another BIG CHANGE. Choosing to give up alcohol... BIG CHANGE. But for you, it may be something different. It may be walking away from the job that's sucking the life out of you. It could be leaving the city you're currently living in because things haven't worked out as planned. Maybe it's moving back home, allowing yourself the necessary humility to live with supportive family and friends as you choose a new direction. Maybe it's leaving college to pursue a different career path that's better suited for your creativity and gifts. Maybe it's moving out of the city where your ex lives in order to distance yourself from residual pain.

These BIG changes to our "environment" allow us to pivot, and break free from major external forces keeping us from *finding better*; they shake everything up. Both Depression and Anxiety can linger if we remain in the same environment that continually produces the same triggers.

I'm not encouraging you to make an immediate, rash decision. Don't quit your job tomorrow simply because of this chapter! Think it through, make a plan, and seek support.

———————————

The well-known definition of insanity often attributed to Albert Einstein is, "doing the same thing over and over again and expecting different results." Take that quote and compare it to your current environment. Maybe no matter how hard you strive to change, living in the *same* environment is keeping you from seeing different results. Your environment has to be conducive for positive self-growth; it has to be a launching pad for your new pursuit of *finding better*.

We would never advise someone trying to lose weight to work at McDonald's.

We would never tell a person struggling with low self-esteem post break-up to hop on Tinder.

We would never direct a person bogged down in debt to open another credit card.

When I gave up alcohol, it would have been foolish for me to live in a fraternity house. That environment would have contradicted my new choice.

BIG pivots in life feel like ripping a Band-Aid off your skin. Whether or not we like to admit it, many times the comfort of staying in a familiar environment feels like it outweighs the underlying toxicity. But it doesn't. Pivoting is removing yourself from an environment that's holding you back.

Making these pivots isn't fun. Few things in life are as scary as committing to a full-on change of direction. Know that it's okay to be unhappy about leaving an "environment" behind. Rarely do we grant that permission to ourselves. Let nostalgia and uncertainty have its place, but then *own* your decision. Be expectant and excited to grow in new soil.

TAKEAWAYS

- Sometimes *finding better* requires more than just pure self-improvement; it can require BIG CHANGE.
- While "pivoting" may be the right choice, it doesn't mean it will be easy.
- *Own* your pivot, and trust that what you're doing is the right thing.

THE MAN OF STEEL

· BEING AUTHENTIC ·

By this point in the book, you may have noticed that I've begun most chapters with a story or analogy. Throughout the writing process, I purposefully toyed with many awkward, and humorous stories/examples to find the ones I thought would be the most relatable.

One of the most impactful mentors in my life has the same approach when he speaks. He lays out his imperfections, awkwardness, and funny encounters in hopes of further connecting with his audience.

I must admit I'm far from capable of doing this with the ease that he does. But every week, I question why I hesitate at times to be fully authentic in my interactions and endeavors. As I mentioned earlier in the book, the interesting thing about authenticity is that when it's practiced, *perfection* (or the idea of it) walks straight out the door, and in its place, *peace* walks in.

Authenticity reaches beyond just being able to be comfortable in your own skin. It's speaking truthfully about the events happening in one's life.

Occasionally, this mentor of mine approaches giving advice without the bumper of a funny story. Rather, he's brutally honest about his life. He openly shares his struggles, and how he's walking through them, to encourage those who may be feeling similarly to him.

So, with the intention of being my most authentic self with you, I have decided to write this last chapter without the cushion of a funny story. Instead, I want to let you look even deeper into my life, hoping that you (or someone you know) can relate to my struggles. I've opened up this much about my life, I might as well go all the way!

Writing this book has been the biggest priority of my life for some time now.

After I knocked out the first chapter, I sat back more confidently, believing that I could manage to write the rest of the book with ease. But, as many writers have felt, my confidence dwindled as time went on. My words started to dry up, my desire started to deflate, and my thoughts began to wage war with my initial positivity. The book became a humbling ride, exposing areas of my life that I thought had previously healed.

I can sit here and truthfully say that the "boy" I was three years ago during my darkest season doesn't even resemble the "man" I am today. I also don't believe I'll ever feel that low again. I know that the biggest part of my healing process has occurred. I've made all the "moves" in this book, and because of that consistent approach, I stand here today alive, healthy, and with a profound sense of purpose and meaning over my life.

However, at multiple times throughout writing this book, Depression and Anxiety came charging back at me in an attempt to tackle my dream. Consequently, there were periods along this journey that were reminiscent of my past struggles, mirroring the feelings that once overwhelmed me.

One of these periods occurred midway through writing the book. I was seriously beginning to doubt my ability to finish the second half.

I was working as a part-time personal trainer in Denver; one of the country's most expensive cities. I was barely able to pay my rent, utilities, and groceries. I felt pressured to pivot in a new "career" direction. Anxiously, I dropped all the momentum I had (or what was left of it), and I started applying for marketing jobs.

I was so anxious about my future and finances that I let thoughts of worry take over my mind, dropping my dream. For a couple of months, I submitted a bunch of job applications with hopes of ending my Anxiety. I felt sure that I didn't have what it would take to be an entrepreneur. Despite my efforts, no opportunities opened up. For whatever reason, the universe, a higher power, destiny, (I call it God), wasn't going to let me get off that easy.

After a weekend of back-and-forth thoughts and wise counsel from my family, I paused the job search process and reengaged with finishing the book.

So, for those of you with a dream, I want to reassure you that *seeing it through is worth a season of scarcity.*

My second awful period was more likely the culmination of weeks of off-track thinking. As many of you know, Depression and Anxiety can build up. Like Lego bricks in the hands of an insistent child, Depression and Anxiety lay pieces over time to eventually create an intimidating wall of negativity and doubt. They sneak up on us if we're not careful, and that's precisely what happened to me. I let my mind shift back to old thought-patterns that sent me back down the path of feeling depressed and anxious. My internal thoughts were charged by external pressures, creating a small-scale storm; one that was powerful enough to develop significant

Depression and Anxiety. It all came to a head one day, about three-quarters of the way through writing this book.

I couldn't get out of bed. I couldn't eat. I couldn't get myself to workout. I couldn't break the stream of negative thoughts. I couldn't find my faith. Mid-day, I sat down slumped on my tiny kitchen floor with tears filling my eyes. In that moment, I wondered why these thoughts were coming with such relentless force. I felt hopeless and completely drained of any motivation. I stood up and walked over to my mirror. Looking at myself, I immediately felt defeated. I thought: *I can't believe you're not stronger than this. What's wrong with you?* Ironically, I felt the powerfully self-deflating shame that comes with writing a "self-help" book when I, myself, felt like I was the one who needed the most help at that moment.

I share all of this with you so that as you go on to pursue becoming a better version of yourself, and conquer Depression and Anxiety, you'll realize that we're all bound by this limitation called the "human condition." I wish I wasn't an imperfect human with wavering confidence and vulnerable thoughts, but this is the challenging reality for all of us. I wish I was Superman!—full of energy and strength, courageously showing up in the face of danger at the drop of a hat.

But, I'm not.

The closest that I'll ever get to that level of impenetrability is by dressing up as Clark Kent for Halloween, wearing my non-prescription frames and slightly shabby, light grey suit. However, I've reminded myself that I shouldn't jump to conclusions about my wish to be invincible. If you know anything about comics, then you know that even Superman has a weakness; he's not perfect either. When exposed to kryptonite, he becomes weak.

The reality is that sometimes we face situations in life that mirror the crystals of kryptonite.[1]

Whether it be our:
- exhausted/stressed mind and body
- stretched finances
- sudden loss
- the process to reach a dream
- complications with our health
- loneliness or singleness
- dissatisfaction with ourselves
- unchecked substance use
- or, the presence of toxic people in our life

... individual crystals of kryptonite align and attempt to *destroy our confidence...* and with it, ultimately *our calling*.

If the story ended here — with total defeat — then that would be quite disappointing! Why would we even want to read about Superman? What's the point if kryptonite wins out every time?

But, the story doesn't end there...

I'm not a comic book expert, but from what I've seen with the history of Superman, somehow, he always finds a way to overcome his weakness and save the day. In the same way, don't you dare believe that you were merely meant to succumb to the kryptonite in your life. You and I are *capable* of walking forward with our weaknesses, having the mindset that each trial will only *empower us further* as we continue our journey.

Let me go back to what happened on that awful second bout of Depression and Anxiety...

I did my best to get through my scheduled personal training sessions. Then, I let someone know that I was "in a funk" and struggling. I let that family member "speak life" over me via a phone call. And even though I felt incapable of doing anything — not even moving — I forced my body to get outside and go for a walk. I went to get my favorite food (S/O Chipotle — you have my heart). I rested. I turned on Netflix in an attempt to distract my thoughts. And then... I rested some more. Most importantly, I didn't allow any unnecessary pressures to creep in convincing me to "accomplish more," "be stronger," or "feel magically better." I was determined to not let these types of self-worth based thoughts cloud my simple steps back toward normality. Instead, I allowed myself to live with the heightened inadequacy I temporarily felt until I had weathered that storm.

When Depression or Anxiety stand on the doorstep knocking, this is sometimes all that you can do. Sure, it was a grueling stretch that knocked the emotional wind out of me, but I got through it.

———————

You must understand that during this new path you choose to take, there will be setbacks and trials. There will be moments where you feel like you've made a mistake, or that you've taken a step back. You may feel like you'd rather go back to the old way you were living life—convinced that the hard work isn't worth it. You may even feel like you are losing the energy to fight. But, you must know that these feelings are part of living in a continual state of imperfection (a.k.a. the human condition). If we were perfect beings, then we wouldn't struggle with anything!

I implore you to do what I have done many times in my life... *keep taking small steps forward*, no matter how small. Your direction and intention will determine your ability to make it to a new destination.

This is the all-important habit I talked about in the last chapter: continually getting back up after moments, days, or weeks where you get knocked down. It's a specific mindset that you must develop to never settle for a life directed by Depression and Anxiety. Rather, let your life be dictated by the choice to keep showing up every day, striving to be the best that you can be. Show up with the intention to live an exceptional life even though there will *most definitely* be a few speed bumps along the way.

Forget super strength or the ability to fly, this deeply seeded determination to walk with our imperfections and through any struggles we face is the actual definition of a superhero.

No cape needed.

TAKEAWAYS

- Even Superman, "The Man of Steel," has an area of weakness.
- Perfection is impossible. Persistence is possible.
- Do you remember the final statement of this book's introduction? Let's take it full circle: *Sometimes, just showing up is a victory.*

THERE IS NO MAP

· CONCLUSION ·

Building on the concept that I introduced at the very beginning of this book, there are many roads in life that can be taken. Some veer to the left, some to the right. Some are narrow, and some are wide. Some are perfectly paved, and some are cracked and bumpy. On some, you're meant to go fast, and on some, you're meant to go slowly. And almost every road leads to another, and then another, and then another. But even with all of these options, and directions, and venturesome possibilities, there's not a single map that can accurately predict what the end destination will look like.

This is the big challenge for all of us. There's nothing more daunting than heading off to travel without a map… but, that's life.

How will I know what my life will look like? How will I know which ways to go? How will I know that the end I'll reach will be all that I had hoped for?

There may not be a customized map for each of us to solve this ambiguous reality, but I do believe that there is a surefire approach that will lead to what we long for—a dynamic story full of purposeful impact and rewarding adventure.

The truth is, if you're headed in the right direction—if you feel deep in your heart that you're pursuing *better*—then you'll make it to where you hope to go. You'll look back and see lots of twists and turns. You'll see moments where you had to make a change of direction to get on another road. You'll see moments where you needed to pull over and rest. You'll see moments where you wished you had taken a different turn, and you'll see moments where you picked the perfect route that led to many others.

You'll drive under beautiful blue skies and toward bold, brilliant sunsets. And yet, you'll also have to drive through the dark of night. You'll have to drive through rain, mud, hail, and sleet. These stretches will inevitably scratch up your exterior, and you may feel more vulnerable than usual in these moments. However, like anybody who has ever been on a long road trip knows, the scenery never stays the same for too long.

Work to maintain your car. Life is a long trip, and you're going to need to take care of your vehicle to make it to the end.

——

As for any car troubles that you may run into (a.k.a. Depression, Anxiety, insecurities, eating disorders, shame, addiction, loss, etc.), never attempt to just cover up them with a fresh coat of paint. Dig deep, find help, and be open to doing serious work on all the parts of your car, including the engine (a.k.a. your mind). Learn how your engine runs so that you can better react when something feels off. No engine is perfect, and no engine can work indefinitely without needing repairs. That's the commonality between all of us who are traveling, even if you can't always see it.

And quite frankly, don't worry so much about the big picture. The conscious ability to enjoy the drive is honestly way more important than *overthinking* and *obsessing* about any "destination."

All of this is to say, as you head off to *find better*, know that there is no map—there never will be. But the thing is, you don't need a map to *find better*. All you need is determined intentionality to head off in a *better* direction. Make the next best decision that's in front of you...

The rest will take care of itself.

The END

... is just

the

beginning.

ACKNOWLEDGEMENTS

To this date, nothing has challenged me more than writing this book. From an outsider's perspective, a book seems merely like words strung together, pages bound, and copies printed.

However, for anyone who has ever dared to engage with this form of communication, they know this is no small feat. Behind this book, stands a community of people who have helped inspire me, lead me, and guide me.

First and foremost, thank you, parents. For all that you do, and for your endless support to chase down this calling.

Thank you, Suzanna. You are the world's best sister, and my go-to advisor.

Thank you to the rest of my family for your support and years of love.

To my inner circle (you know who you are): Thank you for your prayers, accountability, and encouragement. I can't wait to make more memories with this crew! I'm beyond blessed to have met you all.

Thank you to my editors: Sharon Coil, Judith Snyder, and Tom Tafoya. Thank you for the hours spent helping me mold my thoughts into meaningful conclusions.

Gary Bender, thank you for your investment in my life. Thank you for your unending support in more than a few of my endeavors. Thank you for the many hours spent editing as well. This would not have happened without you!

Kelley Gray... you are one of a kind. Thank you for your counsel during my storm.

Thank you to all of the Red Rocks Church Pastors and Staff. Thank you to some of the most influential spiritual leaders in my life: Chad Bruegman, Shawn Johnson, Jessie Davis, Doug Wekenman, Andrew Matrone, Connor Grim, and Ronnie Johnson. This book is proof that your messages touch the entire church. Also, thanks to Robert Gelinas, Carl Lentz, and Levi Lusko for being three other spiritual leaders I continue to glean wisdom from.

Thank you, Seth Godin, for the incredible art you have created. Your books have changed the way I look at marketing, and quite frankly, life.

Thank you, Scotty Bates, for being an amazing, supportive freshman roommate.

And thank *you* for reading this book. I hope *FINDING BETTER* impacts your life.

RESOURCES/
ENDNOTES

These resources can help you *find better* and improve your mental health. Maybe you need to talk to someone right now. Maybe finding a long-term counselor is the best move. Maybe you just want to read another book to keep growing toward *finding better*. Regardless, there's something here that can help you.

RESOURCES

National Suicide Prevention Lifeline: 1-800-273-8255

*I heard an advocate for mental health and suicide prevention pose the question, "Do you really want to die, or do you just want the way you're feeling to stop?" That question is the root of all suicidal thoughts. In almost all cases, a person's true answer is the latter... and finding that relief is possible with the right help and approach. Don't stop until you find that.

National Alliance on Mental Illness (A non-profit trying to end mental health stigmas. They offer support and resources to help guide you toward better mental health.): **www.nami.org**

Active Minds (A non-profit initiative to end young adult mental health stigmas on college campuses. Support groups are active on 450+ campuses): **www.activeminds.org**

The Trevor Project (LGBTQ Young Adult Mental Health — Trained counselors are there to support people 24/7 for a safe and judgment-free place to talk.): **1-866-488-7386 or Text "START" to 678678 - www.thetrevorproject.org**

Talk Space (Online counseling with thousands of specialized counselors and therapists to choose from. It is online counseling streamed directly from your smartphone.) **www.talkspace.com**

*If you're a college or high school student, also look into your school's counseling center and the support they offer. School counselors can be an open ear and someone to discuss the stresses of being a student with.

AA (Alcoholics Anonymous is a nationwide support system for people looking to overcome drug and alcohol addictions. Small groups meet to support each other and share their experiences to help each other develop healthier habits.): **www.aa.org**

Celebrate Recovery (Faith-based 12-step recovery program for anyone struggling with hurt, pain or addiction.): **www.celebraterecovery.com**

Erika's Lighthouse (An organization dedicated to helping adolescents and teenagers cope with depression.): **www.erikaslighthouse.org**

Girl Above (Girl Above is a grassroots non-profit organization dedicated to empowering and equipping girls to live authentically and confidently. Resources for young women facing depression, insecurity, anxiety, loneliness, bullying, and more.): **www.girlabove.com**

PERSONAL SUGGESTIONS/ RESOURCES

ACNE PROGRAMS
Face Reality: **www.facerealityacneclinic.com**
Natural Acne Clinic: **www.naturalacneclinic.com**

FAITH
Red Rocks Young Adults Messages:
www.rrya.org
Red Rocks Church Messages:
www.redrockschurch.com/media/

Fresh Life Church Messages:
www.freshlife.church/messages/

BOOKS
Embracing imperfection and finding authenticity:
The Gifts of Imperfection by Brené Brown

Opening up, letting go, and finding the courage to
be vulnerable with others about your struggles:
Daring Greatly by Brené Brown

Living an exceptional life (spiritual): *Own the
Moment* by Carl Lentz

Developing creativity, finding a fulfilling career,
and becoming indispensable in that career field:
Lynchpin by Seth Godin (My all-time favorite book)

Drug and alcohol habits/addiction and the science
behind it. Why are we so drawn to them?: *Never
Enough* by Judith Grisel

Nutritional guidance and the power behind healthy
eating habits: *It Starts with Food* by Melissa Hartwig

The importance of sleep, and how to achieve better
sleep: *Why We Sleep* by Matthew Walker

Dealing with loss: *Through the Eyes of a Lion* by Levi
Lusko

——

Cultivating a deep life and a new perspective on career-based success: *The Second Mountain* by David Brooks

Fostering genuine confidence and ignoring the lies that our culture tells women (and men) to believe about themselves: *Girl Wash Your Face* by Rachel Hollis

Financial responsibility and becoming debt free: *The Total Money Makeover* by Dave Ramsey

EMAIL: CONNECT@FINDINGBETTER.ORG

"

Sometimes, just showing up is a victory.

"

LOVE. PEOPLE. WELL.

INSTAGRAM

@ThisIsFindingBetter

FREE. ALL OF IT. ALWAYS.

THE APP

FINDING BETTER

A CONTENT BASED APP

BET TER

DIGITAL BOOK

AUDIOBOOK

RESOURCES

#FINDINGBETTER

Available on the
App Store

ANDROID APP ON
Google Play

SPEAKING

LET'S
LET'S
LET'S
CONNECT
CONNECT
CONNECT

REACH OUT AT...
WWW.FINDINGBETTER.ORG/SPEAKING

FINDING BETTER
FINDING BETTER
FINDING BETTER
FINDING BETTER

WHATCHA THINK?

// LEAVE A REVIEW

IF YOU GOT SOMETHING FROM
FINDING BETTER, THEN PLEASE
LEAVE A REVIEW ON AMAZON.
YOUR FEEDBACK HELPS
OTHERS FIND THIS BOOK.
–THANK YOU

ENDNOTES
PART I: A STARTING POINT

"Will I Ever Feel Like Me Again?"
1) Wolverton, Brad. "As Students Struggle With Stress and Depression, Colleges Act as Counselors." The New York Times, The New York Times, 21 Feb. 2019, www.nytimes.com/2019/02/21/education/learning/mental-health-counseling-on-campus.html.

2) Winerman, Lea. *American Psychological Association*, American Psychological Association, Sept. 2017, www.apa.org/monitor/2017/09/numbers.

3) "Mind Games." *Subsplash.com*, https://subsplash.com/redrockschurch/join-the-team/mi/+8e0471d (google "Mind Games: Depression Red Rocks)
&
4) ibid (To this day, this is the best spiritual message I have heard about Depression. I may have listened to it 8 or 9 times by now. I take no credit for the term "equal opportunity offender," or for the point that well-known influencers/celebrities/artists struggle with depression and anxiety too, therefore it has no bias. These points are Chad Bruegman's conclusions, but have greatly impacted my perspective on seasons of struggle.)

Defining Depression (In A Real Way)
1) "Depression." Merriam-Webster, Merriam-Webster, www.merriam-webster.com/dictionary/Depression.

2) Kannal, Samantha. "Anxiety and Depression: It's Not a Phase." *The Odyssey Online*, Odyssey, 31 Aug. 2017, www.theodysseyonline.com/Anxiety-and-Depression-its-not-phase. (modified slightly for grammatical reasons)

Defining Anxiety (Depression's Best Friend)
1) GOD, CHARLAMAGNE THA. *SHOOK ONE: Anxiety Playing Tricks on Me.* ATRIA BOOKS, 2019.

2) StoryBrand.com. "Building a StoryBrand with Donald Miller: #169: Rebekah Lyons-The Magic of 'Less' to Manage Stress on Apple Podcasts." *Apple Podcasts*, 7 Oct. 2019, podcasts.apple.com/us/podcast/169-rebekah-lyons-the-magic-of-less-to-manage stress/id1092751338?i=1000452614311.

PART II: THE MIND

Vanilla Or Chocolate (Thought Management)
1) "Absolute Words." *Austin Community College*, www.austincc.edu/health/ttt/determination.html.

2) "Train Your Mind To Win With MMA Champion Mike Chandler." *The School of Greatness Podcast by Lewis Howes*, 9 May 2018, lewishowes.com/podcast/train-your-mind-to-win-with-mma-champion-mike-chandler/.

3) Loder, Vanessa. "How To Rewire Your Brain For Happiness." Forbes, Forbes Magazine, 7 Jan. 2016, www.forbes.com/sites/vanessaloder/2015/03/18/how-to-rewire-your-brain-for-happiness/.

Packaging Perfection (Social Media)
1) "Eiffel Tower Key Stats : the Tower in Numbers." *La Tour Eiffel*, 5 Oct. 2018, www.toureiffel.paris/en/the-monument/key-figures.

2) Flannery , Mary Ellen. "As Teen Suicide Rate Increases, States Look to Schools to Address Crisis." *NEA Today (National Education Association)*, 6 June 2018, neatoday.org/2018/05/14/teen-suicide-prevention/.

3) Bartlett, Steven, director. *MENTAL HEALTH. DEPRESSION & INSTAGRAM.* YouTube, 19 Jan. 2018, www.youtube.com/watch?v=BzH0Chm6e9I.

4) Meet Gen z: the Social Generation.Hill Holliday's ORIGIN Market Research Report, Dec. 2017, genz.hhcc.com/hubfs/Gen%20Z%20-%20The%20Social%20Generation%20%7C%20Hill%20Hollida y-4.pdf?submissionGuid=e1937055-9a4a-400f-a5ab-f910a8b6fdbb.

The Pressure Is Good For You
1) Cohen, Roger. "The Harm in Hustle Culture." *The New York Times*, The New York Times, 2 Feb. 2019, www.nytimes.com/2019/02/01/opinion/burnout-hustle-culture-gentrification-work.html.
&
Abeyta, Lisa. "How 'Hustle Culture' Harms Entrepreneurs." *Inc.com*, Inc., 5 Feb. 2019, www.inc.com/lisa-abeyta/why-killing-it-may-be-killing-you.html.

2) Curtin, Melanie. "Why Millennials Feel More Pressure to Succeed Than Any Other Generation." *Inc.com*, Inc., 27 Apr. 2016, www.inc.com/melanie-curtin/why-millennials-feel-more-pressure-to-succeed-than-any-other-generation.html.

3) "Media." Red Rocks Church, www.redrockschurch.com/media/. (The message that this reference comes from could not be specifically found, but it is attributed to a Red Rock's message.)

4) "Media." Red Rocks Church, www.redrockschurch.com/media/. ("Love people well" is a line that's attributed to Chad Bruegman of Red Rocks Church. The specific message could not be found.)

To Dallas And Back

1) "Mind Games." *Subsplash.com*, subsplash.com/redrockschurch/join-the-team/ms/+0d00e33.

2) "Obscurity | Definition of Obscurity in English by Oxford Dictionaries." *Oxford Dictionaries | English*, Oxford Dictionaries, en.oxforddictionaries.com/definition/obscurity.

3) Red Rocks Young Adults, and Jessie Davis. *Pillow Talk: Turn Their Heads*. *YouTube*, YouTube, 1 Sept. 2017,www.youtube.com/watch?v=7JlTYLbpfDM&list=PLtE76 D3kimZf3ZEWbSac0BwyfZkvdikml.

4)"Frivolous | Definition of Frivolous in English by Oxford Dictionaries." *Oxford Dictionaries | English*, Oxford Dictionaries, en.oxforddictionaries.com/definition/frivolous.

5) "Chapter Twenty-One: The Most Unexpected Turn Of Events." The Second Mountain: the Quest for a Moral Life, by David Brooks, Random House, 2019, p. 238.

PART III: THE BODY

She Said, "Hi!"

1) Small, Gary. "Can Exercise Cure Depression?" *Psychology Today*, Sussex Publishers, 25 Sept. 2010, www.psychologytoday.com/us/blog/brain-bootcamp/201009/can-exercise-cure-Depression.

2-4) ibid

5) Mulpeter, Kathleen. "These Are the Best Exercises for Anxiety and Depression." *Health.com*, 24 Mar. 2016, www.health.com/Depression/these-are-the-best-exercises-for-Anxiety-and-Depression.

6-10) ibid

Additional Related Sources for more Information:

Achilleos, Konstantia. "How Hiking Is Good for Your Wellness and Mental Health." *Thrive Global*, Thrive Global, 19 June 2018, thriveglobal.com/stories/how-hiking-is-good-for-your-wellness-and-mental-health/.
&
Harvard Health Publishing. "Yoga for Anxiety and Depression." *Harvard Health Blog*, Harvard Health Publishing, 9 May 2019, www.health.harvard.edu/mind-and-mood/yoga-for-Anxiety-and-Depression.
&
Dregni, Michael. "This Is Your Brain on Exercise." *Experience Life*, Experience Life, 1 May 2018, experiencelife.com/article/this-is-your-brain-on-exercise/.
&
Reynolds, Gretchen. "Meditation Plus Running as a Treatment for Depression." *The New York Times*, The New York Times, 16 Mar. 2016, well.blogs.nytimes.com/2016/03/16/meditation-plus-running-as-a-treatment-for-Depression/.

A Gift From Granny Franny

1) Tello, Monique. "Diet and Depression." *Harvard Health Blog*, Harvard Health Publishing, 22 Feb. 2018, www.health.harvard.edu/blog/diet-and-Depression-2018022213309.

2) Stoller-Conrad, Jessica. "Microbes Help Produce Serotonin in Gut." *The California Institute of Technology*, 9 Apr. 2015, www.caltech.edu/about/news/microbes-help-produce-serotonin-gut-46495.

3) Knapton, Sarah. "Depression Is a Physical Illness Which Could Be Treated with Anti-Inflammatory Drugs, Scientists Suggest." *The Telegraph*, Telegraph Media Group, 8 Sept. 2017, www.telegraph.co.uk/science/2017/09/08/Depression-physical-illness-could-treated-anti-inflammatory/.
&

Rogan, Joe, and Rhonda Patrick. *Depression - SSRI's or Nutrition and Exercise? YouTube*, YouTube, 14 Jan. 2018, www.youtube.com/watch?v=mnA_CNYU3yc&t=675s.

4-6) ibid

Say Yes...
1) Iyer, Apart. "Why Do I Always Feels so Paranoid and Anxious When I Have a Hangover?" *Women's Health*, June 2018, pp. 22–22.

2) ibid

3) Carroll, Linda. "Teen Pot Smoking Raises Risk of Depression in Adulthood, Study Finds." *NBCNews.com*, NBCUniversal News Group, 13 Feb. 2019, www.nbcnews.com/storyline/legal-pot/teen-pot-smoking-raises-risk-Depression-adulthood-study-finds-n971356.

4) ibid

5) Stoner, Susan A. *Effects of Marijuana on Mental Health: Anxiety Disorders*. University of Washington, June 2017, adai.uw.edu/pubs/pdf/2017mjAnxiety.pdf.
&
Arango, Manny. "The RED Conference." 2019.

6) Aubrey, Allison. "Anxiety Relief Without The High? New Studies On CBD, A Cannabis Extract." NPR, NPR, 23 Apr. 2018, www.npr.org/sections/health-shots/2018/04/23/604307015/anxiety-relief-without-the-high-new-studies-on-cbd-a-cannabis-extract.

7) "Can CBD Help with My Anxiety and Depression?" Anxiety and Depression Association of America, ADAA, ADAA, June 2019, adaa.org/understanding-anxiety/cbd.

Milligrams And Misconceptions

1) Parks, Eric. "Anger - Mind Games." Subsplash.com, Red Rocks Church, 9 Aug. 2015, subsplash.com/redrockschurch/join-the-team/mi/+f3be740.

2) Carr, Teresa. "Too Many Meds? America's Love Affair With Prescription Medication." Consumer Reports, Consumer Reports, 3 Aug. 2017, www.consumerreports.org/prescription-drugs/too-many-meds-americas-love-affair-with-prescription-medication/.

3) Archer M.D., Dale. "Vitamin D Deficiency and Depression." Psychology Today, Sussex Publishers, 13 July 2013, www.psychologytoday.com/us/blog/reading-between-the-headlines/201307/vitamin-d-deficiency-and-Depression.

4) Head N.D., Kathi. "Who Is at Risk for Magnesium Deficiency?" Thorne Magazine, 12 Jan. 2018, www.thorne.com/take-5-daily/article/who-is-at-risk-for-magnesium-deficiency.

Exhausted Pigeons

1) "How Much Sleep Do We Really Need?" National Sleep Foundation, www.sleepfoundation.org/excessive-sleepiness/support/how-much-sleep-do-we-really-need

2) Gross, Terry. "Sleep Scientist Warns Against Walking Through Life 'In An Underslept State'." HPPR, July 2018, www.hppr.org/post/sleep-scientist-warns-against-walking-through-life-underslept-state-0. (certain parts changed for grammatical accuracy)

3) Gilger, Lace. "Everything You Know About Sleep Is Wrong with Dr. Matthew Walker." *The Science of Success Podcast*, The Science of Success Podcast, 4 Jan. 2018, https://www.successpodcast.com/show-

notes/2018/1/3/everything-you-know-about-sleep-is-wrong-with-dr-matthew-walker?rq=matthew%20walker.

4,6,7) ibid

5) Walker, Matthew P. *Why We Sleep: Unlocking the Power of Sleep and Dreams*. Scribner, an Imprint of Simon & Schuster, Inc., 2018. Quote found online, but sourced directly from Walker's book.

PART IV: THE SOUL

A Foreword To Faith
1) "Soul | Definition of Soul in English by Oxford Dictionaries." *Oxford Dictionaries | English*, Oxford Dictionaries, en.oxforddictionaries.com/definition/soul.

2) "Soul Synonyms." *Www.thesaurus.com*, www.thesaurus.com/browse/souls.

3) The NIV. Zondervan Bible Pub., 1983. Hebrews 11:1

Highway 34 (Is There More?)
1) Howell, Elizabeth. "How Many Stars Are In The Universe?" *Space.com*, Space.com, 18 May 2017, www.space.com/26078-how-many-stars-are-there.html.

2) Moskowitz, Clara. "What's 96 Percent of the Universe Made Of? Astronomers Don't Know." *Space.com*, Space.com, 12 May 2011, www.space.com/11642-dark-matter-dark-energy-4-percent-universe-panek.html.

Perfectly Imperfect
1) *Holy Bible: New International Version, John 3:16*. Zondervan, 2018.
&
THE MESSAGE BIBLE, Romans 3:23-26. NAVPRESS Publishing Group, 2013.

&
Holy Bible: New International Version, Isaiah 53:5. Zondervan, 2018.

2) *Holy Bible: New International Version, 1 John 4:8*. Zondervan, 2018.

Facts Only
1) *THE MESSAGE BIBLE, John 4:1-28*. NAVPRESS Publishing Group, 2013.

2) "Word Counts: How Many Times Does a Word Appear in the Bible?" *Christian Bible Reference Site*, www.christianbiblereference.org/faq_WordCount.htm.

3) *Holy Bible: New International Version, 1 John 4:7-9*. Zondervan, 2018.
&
Holy Bible: New International Version, 1 Corinthians 13:4-9. Zondervan, 2018.
&
Holy Bible: New International Version, Romans 8:37-39. Zondervan, 2018.
&
Holy Bible: New International Version, Ephesians 2:4-5. Zondervan, 2018.

4) Daigle, Lauren A, et al. "You Say." *Look Up Child*, Sony/ATV Music Publishing LLC, 2018.

A Moment Of Silence
1) Edwards, Bruce. "List of God's Promises." *Breakthrough* , www.breakthroughforyou.com/resources/promises-of-god-listed/.
&
"Promises of God." *List of Promises*, promises-of-god.com/list_of_promises.

2) *Holy Bible: New International Version, Matthew 7:7-8.* Zondervan, 2018.

3) Matrone, Andrew. *Guys' Nights - Admit Your Weakness. Red Rocks Young Adults,* Red Rocks Young Adults, 2 Nov. 2018, www.rrya.org/listen/2018/11/2/guys-nights-admit-your-weakness.

Why Did This Happen To Me?
1) "Online & In-Person Natural Acne Treatment Specialists." *Natural Acne Clinic,* www.naturalacneclinic.com/.
&
"Face Reality Acne Clinic." *Face Reality Acne Clinic,* facerealityacneclinic.com/.

PART IV: WRAPPING IT ALL UP

Who'd You Vote For? (Forming Habits)
1) "20 Mind-Blowing Stats About the Porn Industry and Its Underage Consumers." Fight the New Drug, 30 May 2019, fightthenewdrug.org/10-porn-stats-that-will-blow-your-mind/.
&
"Teens & Young Adults Use Porn More Than Anyone Else." Barna Group, 2016, www.barna.com/research/teens-young-adults-use-porn-more-than-anyone-else/.
&
Silver, Curtis. "Pornhub 2017 Year In Review Insights Report Reveals Statistical Proof We Love Porn." Forbes, Forbes Magazine, 9 Jan. 2018, www.forbes.com/sites/curtissilver/2018/01/09/pornhub-2017-year-in-review-insights-report-reveals-statistical-proof-we-love-porn/#474b9f6824f5.

2) Clear, James. "How to Change Your Beliefs and Stick to Your Goals for Good." James Clear, 13 Nov. 2018, jamesclear.com/identity-votes.

3) "Oprah's SuperSoul Conversations - Steven Pressfield: Unlock Your Creative Genius." *YouTube*, YouTube, 9 Jan. 2019, www.youtube.com/watch?v=wPbaRVtDTdU.
&
Pressfield, Steven. The War of Art: Break Through the Blocks and Win Your Inner Creative Battles. Orion, 2003.

4) Lentz, Carl. *Own the Moment*. Simon & Schuster Paperback, an Imprint of Simon & Schuster, Inc., 2018.

The Man Of Steel (Being Authentic)
1) Downey, Meg. "The Weird and Wonderful History of Kryptonite." *DC*, DC, 5 Apr. 2018, www.dccomics.com/blog/2018/04/05/the-weird-and-wonderful-history-of-kryptonite

ABOUT ME

BEN CHAMPION

Ben Champion – Author of FINDING BETTER

Ben Champion is a 20-something who... (blah blah blah, enter some stereotypical list of accomplishments). Instead, here's a Q and A to get to know me better.

• *What movie can you watch over and over without ever getting tired of it?*
If we're talking funny movie, then Hot Rod. If we're talking meaningful, then About Time.

- *What "old person" things do you do?*

  I drink coffee black, I can fall asleep in any chair, and I use words like "oopsie" and "darn it!"

- *Which do you like more dogs or cats?*

  Life isn't complete without dogs.

- *What's your guilty pleasure?*

  Reese's (Easter Egg edition — more peanut butter).

- *If you could have an all-expenses paid trip to see any part of the world, where would you go?*

  Scotland is up there. Or Australia.

- *What is the dumbest way you've been injured?*

  Jumping into a pile of snow.

- *What is the most random thing you've ever watched all the way through on Netflix?*

  Jiro Dreams of Sushi.

- *What simple change could you make in your life that would have the biggest positive impact?*

  Calling friends and family on a more regular basis just to catch up.

- *What is the most embarrassing thing you have ever worn?*

  A Ninja Turtles themed toga.

• *What about becoming an adult caught you completely off guard?*

That life is truly hard.

I had heard adults say that my entire life, but I didn't recognize the depth of that statement until I entered my 20s. Of course, there are really good things that we experience (deepening friendships, personal achievements, and new opportunities). But there are also really hard things we face (having to let things and people go, inner-personal battles, and anxiety-inducing uncertainty). "Life" is this awesome, challenging, fun, stressful mixed bag of memories and moments. There are plenty of highs, but with the highs come some lows; no one gets off scot-free. The lows were harder than I expected, but I was equally caught off guard by how they changed my perspective for an even richer life.

Thanks for checking out FINDING BETTER. I hope it impacts your journey.

Best

"We choose the
direction we go in life."

Made in the USA
Coppell, TX
27 October 2019

10548619R00174